D0283264

THE
HAUNTING
—— OF THE ——
TENTH AVENUE
THEATER

© Alex Matsuo

About the Author

Alex Matsuo is an actor, director, and playwright by day, and a paranormal researcher and investigator by night. She has researched and investigated the paranormal for nearly a decade and is the founder of the Association of Paranormal Study, which specializes in private home investigations and consultations with a solutions-based approach. She is the author of *The Haunted Actor*, published in 2014, which is about the relationship between theater and the paranormal. In 2013, Alex was nominated for a Shorty Award for her work in online radio for the paranormal. She currently hosts *The Wicked Domain* for LiveParanormal.com and has previously hosted the shows *ParaNation* and *Paranormal Insider Radio*. She received her master's of arts in theater arts from San Diego State University in 2011 and currently resides in Raleigh, North Carolina.

THE
HAUNTING
— OF THE —
TENTH AVENUE
THEATER

ALEX MATSUO

Llewellyn Worldwide
Woodbury, Minnesota

The Haunting of the Tenth Avenue Theater © 2015 by Alex Matsuo. All rights reserved. No part of this book may be used or reproduced in any manner whatsoever, including Internet usage, without written permission from Llewellyn Publications, except in the case of brief quotations embodied in critical articles and reviews.

First Edition
First Printing, 2015

Book design by Bob Gaul
Cover design by Kevin R. Brown
Cover images by iStockphoto.com/884231/©Soubrette
        iStockphoto.com/9291899/©alengo
        shutterstock/69847318/©HABRDA
Editing by Ed Day
Interior Photos by Jeff Cotta except on pages 143 and 145 by Ann Ryan

Llewellyn Publications is a registered trademark of Llewellyn Worldwide Ltd.

Library of Congress Cataloging-in-Publication Data
Matsuo, Alex, 1986–
  The haunting of the Tenth Avenue Theater/Alex Matsuo.—First edition.
    pages cm
  ISBN 978-0-7387-4560-2
1. Haunted theaters—California—San Diego. 2. Tenth Avenue Arts Center (San Diego, Calif.) I. Title.
  BF1477.5.M38 2015
  133.1'29794985—dc23
                  2015020512

Llewellyn Worldwide Ltd. does not participate in, endorse, or have any authority or responsibility concerning private business transactions between our authors and the public.
  All mail addressed to the author is forwarded, but the publisher cannot, unless specifically instructed by the author, give out an address or phone number.
  Any Internet references contained in this work are current at publication time, but the publisher cannot guarantee that a specific location will continue to be maintained. Please refer to the publisher's website for links to authors' websites and other sources.

Llewellyn Publications
A Division of Llewellyn Worldwide Ltd.
2143 Wooddale Drive
Woodbury, MN 55125-2989
www.llewellyn.com

Printed in the United States of America

DEDICATION

For my rock, my biggest cheerleader, and my best friend. No matter how crazy my ideas were, or how adventurous I became, you supported me and encouraged me to believe in myself.

I love and miss you every minute of every day, Mom (1957–2015).

CONTENTS

ACKNOWLEDGMENTS

First of all, I want to thank Jeff Cotta, the owner of the Tenth Avenue Arts Center, for his willingness and enthusiasm to not only allow my team and me to investigate the building but also being a cultivator of the growing arts scene in San Diego. The theater and paranormal communities of America's Finest City salute you.

Second, I want to thank my team members at the Association of Paranormal Study for going on this crazy journey with me: Beth, Amy, Maeve, Beverly, David, Lina, Jay, Nick, Cheri, and Xavier. Without their support, the ongoing work at the Tenth would not be possible.

Third, I want to thank my family and friends for their outpouring of support; especially to my dear friends Joy, Rommel, Michael, Ann, Shirley, Julia, Lindsay, Mark, and Craig.

From dealing with my late-night complaints of little sleep because of writing to cheering me on when I needed that extra push to finish this project, I owe you all my sincerest gratitude.

To my Uncle Jon, thank you for being there to support me, guide me, and constantly encouraging me to reach for the stars.

To Michael, thank you for being a second father to me and giving me clarity in so many areas of my life.

Finally, to my mother: Your never-ending perseverance is nothing short of inspiring and helps me to continue even when life gets tough.

INTRODUCTION

For most of my life, the unknown has always been waiting around the corner. Why is a woman who has a master's degree in theater writing a book about ghosts and the things that go bump in the night? From an academic perspective, this would be seen as illogical and foolish. But it seemed that, in a way, the paranormal chose me. I don't mean that in a conceited sense, but more in the vein that it has always been involved in my life in one way or another. Now, my mother did her best to keep me away from anything related to ghosts, spirits, witches, or other aspects of the occult. But I couldn't help but be fascinated by it. I had to go to the library to read about the paranormal, but I didn't dare take the books home because I didn't want my mother to find out. I couldn't even read the Goosebumps series at home—I had to borrow the books from friends. I feel bad for my mom today because despite her attempts to keep the paranormal from infiltrating my brain, I still found a way to learn more about it. Now it's such an embedded part of my life that I can't imagine my life without the study of the unknown.

So, when I got involved in theater at the age of eleven, I didn't even know about the myth that theaters were haunted, nor did I realize that San Diego was truly a hotbed for paranormal activity. I just wanted to be on stage. But it wasn't until I did my third show at the Spreckels Theatre in downtown San Diego that I heard the local ghost story about the ballerina who fell to her death from the second-story balcony backstage where all of the dressing rooms sit. Ironically, after learning that story, I was on the lookout for the ballerina and thought I caught a few glimpses of her in the wings while I danced on stage. Just the very idea that I could go and look for ghosts was intriguing. But my fascination with the paranormal started long before, with my fascination with death.

My grandfather died when I was very young, and he and I were very close. However, my time with him was cut short when he had an aneurysm burst in his head along with a stroke. For him to go so quickly and so early in my life, the very idea that he died and I would never see him again, was unfair. And so, at the young age of six, my fascination with death started, and it would open the door for my thirst for knowledge about the afterlife. As fate would have it, I was living in the perfect place.

Not only was San Diego America's Finest City, but it also seemed like America's Most Haunted City on the West Coast. I lived just ten minutes away from the famous Whaley House in Old Town. While I didn't remember much about the history of the building, which was built in 1857, I remembered the ghost stories—but that's a kid for you. It seemed that many of the San Diego ghost stories found their roots in the 1800s and were just as turbulent and fascinating as San Diego's history, including the questionable death and haunting of Kate Morgan at the Hotel Del Coronado in 1892. Then there was the haunting of the William Heath Davis House. William Heath Davis was a San Diego icon as the first man who really moved forward in building downtown at its current location. It has become a major icon not only for the history of the city, but also for the paranormal community in San Diego.

As stated earlier, once I learned of the stigma about theaters being haunted, I always kept an extra eye out for anything weird. But to be honest, I haven't really run into any active haunting in most of the theaters I've worked in. The social stigma of the haunted theater is mainly cliché, and most of the time I wonder if the stories arose from a desire to keep teenagers out of the theaters late at night or if it was an attempt to sell a few extra tickets. However, I did experience subtle things in the theaters I worked in that could easily be missed if you weren't paying attention. For example, I would often see someone sitting in the sound booth in the black box theater on my college campus. Maybe I just assumed someone was there out of habit. Someone is always in the booth during productions. But now, given that I was the assistant house manager, I had the key to many of the rooms and theaters in the drama building and was aware of who had a key and who didn't. I knew I was alone. The first time this happened, I did a double take to see who was in the booth at 11:30 at night, only to see an empty space where I saw the person. I would experience this phenomenon multiple times, and with each occurrence, I would try to debunk myself and look for logical explanations. I suppose the crazy thing started happening when I realized that the mysterious figure that I kept seeing in the booth was the same person each time. I had a much more dramatic experience in my last year as an undergraduate. While I was locking up the theater for the night, I saw a shadow walk into my office. Thinking it was my coworker, I went into the office to say hi and ask what she was doing there so late, but I saw nothing. At first, I stopped to consider the possibility I was hallucinating. Or was I just sleepy? But I was completely awake and aware. I searched the rest of the offices for even just a sign of another person. I was fruitlessly trying to find an explanation that just wasn't there. I knew I saw someone go into my office. This was something that I could no longer ignore, and I wanted to go out and find the answers about the unknown. It was my last straw.

Now we have the Tenth Avenue Arts Center, which is also sometimes referred to as the Tenth Avenue Theater. It has become known as one of San Diego's finest secrets when it comes to haunted locations. It wasn't a publicized haunted location, and for several years, it was tied to a church. I had frequented the building often in my last few years of under-graduate school as an audience member seeing friends and colleagues in productions, and then I was a part of a few pro-ductions performed at the Tenth. From the first time I set foot into the multiple-story building, I knew there was something off about the place. I couldn't put my finger on it. And that was a feeling I hadn't gotten from the other haunted locations before. All I really knew about the Tenth was that it was an older building and it used to be a part of a church. But something truly bizarre was happening inside. And as I reflected back on my experience in my office, I thought, what better place to try to answer these questions about the unknown than the Tenth?

In this book, I will be going over my experiences at the Tenth Avenue Arts Center, from my first few visits to inter-views of others who have experienced paranormal phenom-enon as well as details of my own investigations. If you're looking for scientific proof of the haunting at the Tenth, you may need to look elsewhere. In the case of the Tenth, you will quickly discover that the phenomenon in that space—the unexplainable occurrences that seem to happen on a daily basis—is solely dependent on the testimony of eyewitnesses. The factor of the human experience is continually relevant in the paranormal field because it is that eyewitness testimony that has given us urban legends and local ghost stories. It is the human experience that continues to seek out some sort of proof of the afterlife because we don't want to cease to exist as soon as we die. I will also explore the possibility that perhaps we are creating our own haunting at the Tenth, and what it means for the paranormal future of the building.

One

THE CATALYST

My dealings with the paranormal didn't stay in San Diego. As I traveled with my grandmother to her hometown in Kentucky every summer, not only would I hear stories of strange occurrences in the backwoods, I would also have my own experiences. Oftentimes, my great-grandmother, Mamaw, would sit in her chair in the living room as the walls of the house banged with an unexplained noise. This house was old. My grandmother and her siblings were born in the house in the thirties and forties, and my great-grandfather died right here in his bed. But this noise sounded like someone pounding the walls with their fists. As the banging continued, my eyes filled with tears and my grandmother and Mamaw would be reciting the Lord's Prayer into the night. The next morning, it would be like nothing ever happened—until the night came again. In those backwoods, I have found that the people of that tiny river town have a very simple faith. Not because they aren't intelligent, but because their experiences with the supernatural have solidified their faith in God.

One of the most alarming experiences in Kentucky was late into a stormy night when I was nine years old. As I slept in my room, which was (of course) filled with dolls, I looked at a mysterious hooded figure standing outside my window, unfazed by the thunder, wind, rain, and lightning. During this one particular night, the mattress I was sleeping on tilted sideways. At first, I wasn't bothered because this is what happened when my Mamaw would sleep with me so I wouldn't be scared—which was often. As I slid down the tilted mattress, I expected my Mamaw's sleeping body to stop me from falling off.

But she wasn't there.

I fell straight out of the bed.

In total darkness, except for the flicker of the lightning, I was alone, with the mysterious figure once again looming in front of my window. I never slept in that room by myself again.

Saying Goodbye

Flash forward through my preteen years, and I was now at the prime age of fourteen years old. It was the summer before my freshman year of high school and I continued to perform, both in roles for some of the best shows in San Diego and as part of my high school cheerleading squad. In August of 2000, just a few weeks after her seventieth birthday, my grandmother passed away. On the night she died, it was me, my mother, and my aunt sleeping at the family home. During the last several years of my grandmother's life, my mom and I were living with her. Being the young kid that I was, I had a tendency to leave the lights on after leaving the house or after I went to sleep. My grandmother, God bless her soul, would take her hurting body and crawl up the staircase to turn the light off, and then get after me the next morning about how I was wasting money and energy. On the night that she died, I left the light on again. I didn't do it on purpose, but in the midst of my grief, turning off the stair lights was not a high priority.

The next morning, I went downstairs to find my mom and aunt drinking coffee and looking at me with wide eyes.

"What's wrong?" I asked.

"Did you turn the lights off last night after you went to bed?" my mother asked.

"No … I wasn't even thinking about it," I said.

My mother then looked over at my aunt with a surprised look on her face.

"Why?" I asked.

"Well, you didn't turn the lights off, and your mother didn't turn the lights off," my aunt said.

"And …?"

"I didn't turn the lights off either," my aunt announced.

It seemed that someone paid a visit to the house after she had passed on, and wanted to send a "gentle" reminder to turn the lights off before going to bed. Duly noted, Grandma. This certainly didn't help me avoid the paranormal.

A More Terrifying Experience

Through a series of events, and because I wanted to dedicate more of my time to performing, my mother and I made the decision to homeschool me my senior year. As a seventeen-year-old possessing a valid driver's license and the ability to basically make my own school schedule, this was a prime time to decide to start ghost hunting. It no longer mattered that I was out late, because as long as I got my schooling completed, I got to do the activities I wanted.

Thus began my late-night adventures to Old Town. My usual spots would be the old graveyard down the street from the Whaley House before making the uphill drive to Presidio Park where the earliest settlement of California took place. These late-night treks included asking numerous questions into the darkness, such as asking for a name, gender, how they died—you know, the usual "ghost hunting" type questions. All I had with me was a disposable camera and a tape recorder. Many times I'm sure I spooked myself, though I never thought about much in terms of protecting myself during or after the investigation. I was a careless teenager looking for answers.

I would soon get a wake-up call that would spook me to the point of forcing me to walk away. One night, as I was lying down getting ready to sleep, I closed my eyes. But immediately after that, I felt an intense pressure on my hands, arms, chest, and legs. I couldn't move. I struggled and tried to kick, but something wasn't allowing me to move. I was completely awake, but I had my eyes tightly shut because I didn't want to open them. I opened my mouth to call for my mom, but no sound came out as the pressure on my neck increased. I had no choice; I had to see what was going on.

I opened my eyes, and I saw a woman. Her skin was pitch-black, but she was not African American. Her eyes were slanted as if she was of Asian descent. She had a hood around her head like a nun or a nurse from the 1800s. As I gazed upon her, she had a calm look about her, which made it more terrifying. She was outlined in gold as well. As I tried harder to call for help, I could hear my cat hiss at her. The terrifying woman acknowledged my cat as she put her black hands on my mouth, as if to shush me. The experience lasted about a minute before she disappeared, and I could move and scream again.

For several months, I couldn't sleep in my own bed, or even sleep by myself. I slept with my mom in her bed. From her room, I could see the blackness of my room and a dark figure watching me from the other end of the hall, as if waiting for me to come back. My cat hissed at the room as she walked by, and as soon as my mom witnessed this, she realized that perhaps I wasn't being overly dramatic.

Because my father's side of the family has a rich history in the Greek culture, my mom thought it best to talk to someone at the Greek Orthodox Church. We were given holy water, and numerous people came to my room and prayed in the space. Eventually, I worked up the courage to go back and sleep in that room, but I never slept in complete darkness—not even after the intensity of the attacks diminished.

After I told my mother about my late nights ghost hunting, she told me that something must have followed me home. With that, I decided to stop with the ghost hunting, and the attacks eventually stopped.

After I graduated from high school, I had made a promise to myself that college would be the time that I would quit my immature antics of going ghost hunting and keep the paranormal in the backseat. My amateur moonlighting as a ghost hunter finally caught up with me, and it was time to take an indefinite break. Besides seeing the occasional figure in the sound booth, my paranormal life had gone to sleep. Sometimes it would pop back up, as ghosts were very versatile dramatic tools for plays and musicals, but it would never go deeper than a performance reference. During the times I tried to resist the urge to pick up my flashlight, I would go to the library and dive into some books about the occult. When I would slip, I would call it research.

But the experience in my office shook me enough to where I decided, after my education was over, I would go back to investigating. But I would do it right this time.

Assembling a Team

It would be another two years after the office experience. When I graduated and earned my master's of arts in theater, I found myself diving headfirst back into the paranormal. But this time it was so much more than just going to haunted locations and trying to find a ghost. I wanted to learn more about the history of the locations so that I could at least understand the context of the haunting, much like a dramaturg studies and researches a play to understand the context and protect the integrity of the work. I wanted to start protecting the integrity not only for the historical location that had ghostly tenants, but also the integrity of the deceased. My mind-set about investigating had changed, and I also learned that there were people just like me who were going through a paranormal experience and didn't know what to do about it, let alone where to start in trying to understand and handle the phenomenon. So in 2011, just a few months after graduation, I started the Association of Paranormal Study. I gathered a group of like-minded individuals who wanted to learn more about the paranormal as well as help clients with their unknown occurrences.

The first members to join the team were Jay and Beverly. They were a young couple in their early twenties. Jay was in the military, and Beverly was in school. Both of them were passionate about the unknown, and it was fate that brought us all together. Then I met a motorcycle-riding military man by the name of Tom, who was also seeking a team of like-minded people to investigate the paranormal with. Soon after, Jay asked me if his friend Rick could join as well. Rick was also in the military, and had a good head on his shoulders. Here I was with a total of four team members, three of whom were in the military. It was an interesting team dynamic, and the member's military experience helped set a strict standard of performance and professional conduct.

The primary focus of APS is to take on client cases with a solution as the goal, which means that we investigate to solve problems for clients rather than just collecting evidence or experiencing the "thrill of the hunt." I will say that client casework is much different than investigating a public location. While I enjoy client casework, as it can be very fulfilling and you have a chance at helping members of your community, there is an extraordinary amount of pressure. With the slip of the tongue, you could break up a marriage, destroy trust between families, or send someone into a psychotic break. There are a lot of liabilities when it comes to entering someone's home, and you have to decide if it is worth the risk. Because of the amount of pressure and extra attention to detail that my team goes into with each client, whenever we have an opportunity to investigate a public location, we do it. Not only does it act as practice for our investigation techniques, but it also gives us a moment to have some fun on the field while conducting our research. Interestingly enough, while the pressure of affecting someone's personal life is non-existent while investigating a known public haunted location, the approach is nearly identical.

With this in mind, I had to seek out a place where I could properly train my team members that functioned like a private case, but also allowed for mistakes to be made with little to no consequence. I wouldn't find this place until I fell into it by accident.

Meeting the Tenth

As an actor, you find yourself going from company to company for the sake of finding consistent work. This led to working in many different theaters. One of those theaters included the Tenth Avenue Arts Center. My main experiences working in the theater was with two productions as an actor. This was during my undergraduate time, when I was still scarred by the woman over my bed and had put in a lot of effort to shield and block out anything paranormal. While I felt that I was being watched at the time, I remained focused on my task at hand in the theater. If I saw something out of the corner of my eye, I ignored it. If I heard something weird, I pretended that I didn't hear it. I was willfully ignorant. I only spent a few weeks in the building, and I was always with a large number of people. It was always too chaotic to notice anything out of the ordinary besides what I mentioned. The same went for the times I went to the Tenth to watch a production.

This next venture to the Tenth was different: I was out of school, and my focus was back on the paranormal. I was also focusing on a different project that would require me to spend a lot of time in the theater by myself.

As mentioned earlier, during my undergraduate and graduate school years, the only time I expressed any interest in ghosts was when I was studying a play that used the supernatural to drive the plot. I didn't discuss ghosts or spirits with my social circle, and quite honestly, I was a bit of a wallflower and socially awkward. I had a social life, but it was mediocre. I often found myself working on productions outside of school, which meant that I missed out on socializing with my fellow classmates. Granted, the socializing improved during my final years in school, but basically I was not all that open about myself in school. It took people a long time to get to know me because I wouldn't let them in. But once I started working on client cases, I couldn't expect the people I worked with to be open about their experiences if I couldn't practice what I preached.

Once I got my degree and began to start my career as a teaching artist for theater, I became a bit more open about the paranormal in my life, and it began to take on a powerful presence in my social media world. I had expected to lose some friends or be on the receiving end of jokes. But I was prepared for that possibility. Since I had gotten out of graduate school, I found myself attending numerous performances several times a week in order to support my friends and colleagues. I spent about as much time in these performance venues as if I were in a production of my own. And one of the venues I would end up frequenting the most would be the Tenth Avenue Arts Center, as the building would be utilized by many of my friends from college who were just starting their new theater companies.

The Training Ground

As I stood in front of the Tenth, the ominous tan building loomed over me. The windows were like eyes glaring down at me. I took a moment and looked up at the building and couldn't help feeling like I was being watched. It was very well possible, as there were offices in the upper floors and someone certainly could have been looking down at me. But this was different. There were several eyes peering down at me, just waiting and watching to see what my next move would be. I'll be the first to admit that this wasn't like me. I was always the person who would rationalize feelings like this and attribute them to logical explanations like nerves or something going on psychologically. I wasn't one to automatically think something was paranormal without thoroughly investigating it. So what was wrong here?

With immense unease, I walked across the street to the looming building and rang the doorbell. As I stood at the front door, the feeling that I was being watched increased. After what seemed like several minutes (it was more like thirty seconds), a cheerful man answered the door. He had brown hair, a stubbly beard, and a very friendly smile.

Jeff and I had only been coordinating through e-mail and phone calls for just over two months when it came to booking the Tenth. As Jeff asked me if I was ready, I looked inside the lobby and noticed the entrance to the theater. I stepped in and saw the antique elevator right in front of me and the staircase to my left. I took a quick peek inside the elevator and noticed the original interior was still intact.

I looked at the doors to the theater, and Jeff led me over. Behind the elevator, I noticed an open door to my left that had all of the electrical aspects of the building and a dark ladderlike staircase, which led to the basement. Jeff mentioned that he wanted to turn it into a wine cellar.

I felt really uneasy, so I turned and walked through the open doors. Not realizing I had to make a turn, I ran into a black curtain, which was the back of the seating platform. Embarrassed, I turned to my left, and then an immediate right. And there it was ... the Tenth Avenue Arts Center main stage.

I was currently rehearsing a staged reading of my play, *Japanese Eyes/American Heart*, and the Tenth gave many opportunities to local theaters and playwrights to present new works at an affordable price, a deal I immediately jumped at. At this point, the paranormal was the last thing on my mind.

I always tried to do my best to keep my paranormal interests and my theater career separate, mainly because I didn't want my paranormal work to jeopardize my chances of getting roles in shows or being hired as a dramaturg (also known as the person who does research and "represents" the play). I was well aware that my interests in the unknown could freak people out or, on a more positive note, make interesting drinking stories.

The exterior of the Tenth Avenue Arts Center. Courtesy of Jeff Cotta.

But when I'm in a space that is potentially haunted, I'll admit that my senses are elevated a bit. I'm in no way psychically gifted. I don't see dead people nor can I predict the future in any way. Thanks to the theater's website, I was aware of the ghosts of the Tenth Avenue Arts Center but I was determined to not pay attention. Again, I was there to work on my play, not to investigate a reported haunting.

As Jeff showed me around the theater, I was thinking of the chair layout in my head and how I was going to stage my play, when I noticed movement out of the corner of my right eye. Being that the theater was all curtain on the sides, I immediately assumed that it was the air ventilation moving the fabric around. But as I turned my head to look, it appeared as though someone was walking back and forth on the other side of the curtain.

Immediately, I made a beeline to the moving fabric and placed my hand through the curtain and hit a wall. I looked back at Jeff, who had a grin on his face as he directed me to the light booth up above.

"The only way to turn the lights up and down is to do it from the light booth on the second floor, so you'll need to take the elevator or the stairs," he said as he pointed upward. Looking up to the second-floor light booth, it looked as though someone could have very well been looking down at us.

It was beginning to get more difficult to turn off the paranormal investigator inside me.

I asked Jeff to take me up to the second floor to show me the light board and what I needed to do to work the lights so I could show my helper how to do it on the night of the staged reading. As we walked up the first flight of stairs to the second floor, I began to feel cold chills. It could have also been because I was out of shape.

Jeff got his keys out and mentioned they were needed to access the light booth, so he would leave them for me on the night of the staged reading. As he opened the door, he showed me the tech ropes on working the lights, and I looked down into the audience and the stage.

I turned and Jeff took me back downstairs and gave me the rundown on the lobby, selling refreshments, and where to leave the check and the key once my staged reading was done for the evening. Between rehearsals, getting the theater ready, and running the evening, I had a full plate.

Unexpected Audience Members

Fast-forward to a few days later: As I knocked once more on the large red doors and rang the bell, I had an armful of stuff that I was struggling to keep together. This trip had nothing to do with anything paranormal. This trip to the Tenth was for my staged reading of my play, *Japanese Eyes/American Heart.* I got to the theater early so that I could not only collect myself, but also make sure everything was settled and ready to go by the time my actors arrived. As he opened the door, Jeff welcomed me with his usual smile and handed me the keys to the building. He took me back upstairs to the lighting and sound booth where the board was on and ready to go. The night of the staged reading had arrived. It almost felt surreal.

"Do you have someone to turn down the lights for you?" he asked.

"Yeah, they should be here any time, but go ahead and show me how to turn the lights down, and that way you don't have to wait around," I replied.

I really hated to be a burden to anyone, and since Jeff trusted me enough with the keys and to be in the building by myself, I figured I would try to make life as easy for him as possible.

So Jeff opened up the door to the booth, which looked more like a balcony, and let me play around with the buttons. He showed me how to turn it on, and since I already had experience with using a lighting booth, I discovered that his setup was very similar to the board I used in college. I was able to set my "pre-show" lights where the audience was illuminated and the stage was dark, and once it was showtime, the two spaces traded light so to speak—and the stage was lit and the audience was dark. I was rather pleased with myself at my simple light design. As long as the audience could see the actors, I was happy. This was going to be a simple and humble staged reading. In the back of my mind, I began to grow concerned because I wasn't sure if anyone would actually show up.

"When you're not in here, make sure you lock the door to the booth. There's a good couple grand of equipment in this room, so the door has to remain locked at all times if there's no one in here," Jeff explained.

He wished me luck and left the building. The Tenth was eerily quiet as I got to work setting everything up for the night. But it was just me and the stage.

Or so I thought.

As I set the chairs up, I thought I was the only one in the building except for a few people in the upper floors in their office spaces. As I surveyed the area to set up the chairs in the main stage, I heard a young girl giggling from a direction near the light booth, and I turned around toward the doorway to the lobby and saw no one. Of course at this point, being alone in the theater with no light was a bit nerve-racking. So I quickly grabbed the keys and headed up the stairs so I could bring up the house lights.

At this point, my mother had arrived so she could film the staged reading from the top of the raked seats. She was rather fortunate with her camera since her work accidentally broke her old one and replaced it with a camera that was worth about $8,000. I was still waiting for my help for the lighting booth so I decided to stay in the theater for the time being.

Once the stage was more illuminated and my mother finished setting up, I saw that a few of my actors had arrived early so that they could get acquainted with the space and see how their voices carried in the theater. I watched them rehearse and gave them final notes on the development of each scene, especially a pivotal one toward the end of the play.

As I was waiting, with my two actors on the stage and my mother in the audience getting her camera set up, I felt a little uneasy—like I was being watched. It was an odd feeling since anytime I'm with Jeff, I don't really feel nervous in the theater. In fact, I always feel very safe and secure when he is in the building. I chalked the feelings up to nerves since this was my play's public debut outside of the university setting. I decided to stay in the stage area, and I leaned against the curtain that covered the walls of the theater. I started to feel something against my shoulder that shook me and startled me to the point where I let out a small gasp. I didn't want to interrupt my actors or my mother, so I had to contain any startling reaction I had.

I felt as though someone was trying to dig their hand under my shoulder and back from behind the curtain. As soon as I felt that, I hit the wall with my other hand in an attempt to get whatever that thing was to retract. At first I thought that maybe a mouse or a rat had tried to get under my sweater. Then I moved the curtains to the side and all I saw was wall. I even got out my phone and turned on the flashlight setting and examined the wall and the floor. I even started walking behind the curtain as I looked all over the wall to try to find the source of what scared me. I'm sure my actors thought I was nuts because I was underneath the curtain and then batting at myself and examining the wall as if it had just attacked me. I tried to forget about the experience and continued watching my actors rehearse. But this time I didn't lean against the wall. I tried to learn my lesson after the first time. Getting frightened like this was the last thing I needed, given the importance of this night.

The rest of the acting company arrived soon after, one of which was my team member, Jay. We did a short run-through of a few scenes just so my actors could get their bearings in the space as well as work out some blocking concerns since they were using music stands to hold up their scripts.

While they were running their scenes, from the corner of my eye I could see someone standing in the balcony at the sound booth. Without a second thought, I assumed my helper had finally arrived and had already set up shop.

But then I realized that I still had the key and I had locked the booth per Jeff's instructions.

Immediately, my eyes darted to the balcony above to see who it was, but no one was there. At this point, I really thought I had lost it and was letting the nerves really get to me. So I grabbed my phone to check on my helper. I had two missed calls from her in a span of just a few minutes and several texts with explanations and apologies. Once I realized that she wasn't able to make it tonight because her car broke down, and there was no way that I could go pick her up and be back at the theater in time... I was in despair.

What was I supposed to do now?

At this point, I didn't want to tell my actors that something was very wrong. I didn't want my issues to affect their performances, so I decided on a plan that was a bit crazy.

I decided that I would go ahead and turn the lights down myself after I gave the introduction to the play. Yes, it meant running up the stairs (in heels) to get the job done, but I was going to do it because this was my baby being presented on stage, and I couldn't bear to let any mess ups happen.

The pre-staged reading rehearsal was fairly uneventful besides that little incident and my actors went backstage to get dressed and ready. After getting the comment cards ready for the audience, I stood backstage with my actors as people began to arrive. I finally told them the situation and that I needed their help to make sure the light transition ran smoothly. Several more audience members than I initially thought were piling in and sitting in the house, and I remained to the side so that I could jump up and introduce the play. But with this new problem that I had to deal with, there was no way I could relax. The photographer arrived, and I gave him the lowdown of where to set up and what to take pictures of. Everything was ready to go, and all I had to do was begin.

I instructed my actors to not begin the play until the house lights were turned down and to take their time walking from their chairs to their music stands that held their scripts.

"Don't start until the lights go down," I told them.

They nodded their heads and confirmed that they understood what I was asking. I reassured them that I would be bolting to the booth so that they wouldn't be sitting in awkward silence for several minutes. The board was already on; I just needed to slide the house lights down and turn the stage lights up a little brighter.

With the stage still dark, I stepped forward into the light and looked out into the audience. I was happy to see some familiar faces, but the strangers outweighed my friends and family. I introduced my play to the audience and invited them to give their full critique and feedback to me, as it would help me improve the play.

As I looked out into the audience, I saw a fuller house than I thought, and my nerves were elevating slowly along with my blood pressure. I saw Beverly, smiling with support, with Rick sitting next to her. I introduced the play by telling the audience that the play was based on my grandfather and his story of being a Japanese-American in the Army during World War II and my journey of trying to find myself through finding him. In these two different worlds and eras, both of the main characters were trying to find their identity.

I want to take a moment to note that *Japanese Eyes/American Heart* is loosely based on my relationship with my grandfather, the same one whose passing sparked my fascination with death.

As I closed my curtain speech, I thanked the audience for supporting the play and introduced each actor. As the audience applauded, as soon as I was out of their line of sight, I sprinted to the lobby and headed up the stairs to the second floor with the key to the sound booth in my hand. In a rushed fury, I unlocked the booth and heard something that greatly confused me.

My actors had already started reading. They knew to not start until the lights had gone down ... so why were they reading in the dark? I looked out onto the stage to find that the lights in the audience had already gone down and the stage was illuminated. Based on the lines that I heard, they had started almost immediately after I left the theater to go to the booth. How could this be?

I looked down at the light board, and indeed ... the house lights were already off. I thought that maybe someone did me a favor and turned the lights down for me. But that was impossible. I was looking at the light booth the whole time during my curtain speech and saw no one up there. And how would the stranger have known that I needed help in that matter?

I sat in the booth for several more scenes, looking at the buttons and wondering how in the world the lights could have gone down when there was no one up here to push the button. At that moment, that feeling of being watched returned, and this time it was hovering right above my shoulder. While I felt uneasy, I didn't feel threatened. Between the nerves of the evening and the confusion and chaos that was the lighting booth, I really had a rough night emotionally and physically. I silently thanked whoever and whatever turned the lights down for me and continued to watch my play on the stage from the booth.

Tears filled my eyes as I watched this play unfold and thought about the work that was put in to make it happen.

With the topic of the play in mind, I thought of my grandfather. Some people have hypothesized that maybe it wasn't a Tenth Avenue ghost, but my own grandfather who was giving me a helping hand. I would like to think that my grandparents and other deceased relatives are watching over me, but I also feel that it's a selfish notion to have. I'm sure the afterlife is much more fulfilling and interesting than coming back to the world of the living to check on me.

As the staged reading continued, I decided to go ahead and start sneaking back downstairs. I took in the odd occurrence and slowly made my way back downstairs so that I could watch the rest of the play in utter tension as the audience was watching and judging my work. As I began to question my own sanity while giving the audience comment cards for my play and thinking about the situation with the curtains, the giggling, and the house lights seemingly turning themselves down ... the feeling of being watched returned. Everyone was in the theater, and I was alone in the lobby.

My defense mechanisms began to kick in, so I decided to sit in the aisle on the side of the audience where I could watch and listen to the play without being noticed. I started feeling the vibration of someone walking and sitting next to me. I assumed it was one of my friends who arrived late or another patron who needed help getting to their seat. I turned toward the mystery person to greet them and help them get seated.

No one was there.

At this point, I was getting annoyed. Here I was, presenting my work to the public, and instead of obsessing over what the audience was thinking about my play, I was sitting and wondering which ghost in the Tenth Avenue Arts Center was playing with my head. I didn't know whether to be ecstatic that I was having a paranormal experience that would make any researcher and investigator giddy or utterly ticked off that my focus wasn't in the right place.

I continued to sit to the side of the audience where they couldn't see me. As I listened to the actors' words, which were my own, I closed my eyes and simply listened. At that moment, I felt the presence of someone walking up to me. Because my legs were stretched across the aisle, I pulled them in. I assumed it was an audience member leaving or taking a break. But when I opened my eyes, there was no one there.

As an investigator, I go searching for communication with the deceased and unknown entities. A lot of the time, investigations can be unproductive or debunked with simple logical explanation and reasoning. And I've found that when I go out there and actively look for the paranormal, I don't get a response. But if I go on and live my day-to-day life, the paranormal seems to find me. In the case of my experiences of the Tenth Avenue Arts Center, I wasn't expecting to experience the phenomenon and, in fact, was rather annoyed at the poor timing of the ghosts. I suppose that makes me rather selfish, but when I'm focused on my non-paranormal related work, I don't want the lines to cross.

While I was watching my actors fearlessly wrap up my play, I began to hear some sniffles in the audience, and considering I wrote my play in a way that the ending could bring on a few tears, I was pleased with myself. I was also getting emotional myself since the closing scene was a true reflection of my feelings about the lost memories of my grandfather. Finally, the play was done. As I stood up and walked to the side of the stage to applaud my actors for a job well done, they gestured over to me, and I took a bow. The audience clapped, the actors took their bows, and I took questions from members of the audience who wanted to know more about my process, the choices I made in the play, and general questions about theater.

Luckily, I had some friends watching who helped clean up, and I wasn't alone in the theater for the rest of the night until the very end.

Before they departed, Jay, Beverly, and Rick pulled me aside. They asked me if the theater had a history of being haunted.

"I don't know," I said. "How about you tell me?"

The three of them stuttered, trying to find a place to begin. And all they could tell me was they felt like they were being watched and maybe saw some things, but nothing more. Granted, I had spent a significant amount of time in the building, and this was their very first trip to the Tenth. I wanted to stay mum on the ghost stories to see if maybe they would experience something on their own or notice something odd enough that they wanted to ask me about it.

A New Training Ground

I returned the key and placed my check in the kitchen and went to the front door. Knowing that the door would lock as soon as I shut it, I took one last look around the lobby. I would then do something that was out of character for me in the theatrical environment...

I spoke to the ghosts.

I thanked them for letting me use the space, and thanked whoever it was who turned the lights down for me. It was the first time I had talked to an area without feeling like I was speaking to just air. For the first time, I felt like someone or something was actively listening. It wasn't just a theory that the Tenth Avenue Arts Center was haunted; it was a real experience. And I wanted to go back for more.

I shut the door to the Tenth behind me, and the doors locked. I stood in the dark looking at the front door, with city lights and sounds in my ear, and then at the windows above me. As I latched the door, I heard a gentle hum on the other side, like it was coming from a young girl. I immediately looked up back into the windows.

Even though the windows were dark and I couldn't see anything inside, I knew that they were watching. But I didn't really know who "they" were yet. I felt like I had to find out who they were, because I wanted to communicate with them. This was out of character for me. I was a paranormal investigator and researcher who wanted to learn theories and ideas and help people with their haunting.

I wasn't the investigator who asked, "Give us a sign of your presence." I was one who went in already knowing a name and engaging in conversation with the presence. I wasn't one to actively go out and want to get in touch with the deceased just for the thrill of the experience. I was usually one to keep cool, observe, and let them "just be" unless there was a situation where I had to intervene or if I had more information in hand. I didn't recognize this person I was becoming and to be honest, it alarmed me.

As I made the short walk back to my car, I began to think about what the next steps would be to properly investigate the Tenth.

After I got into the car, I looked over at the building one last time and gave it a nod of respect before turning on the ignition and driving away. Oddly enough, I felt like the building was saying, "See you soon" to me, and I looked forward to meeting there again. With so much history associated with the building, I would be more surprised if there wasn't a ghost or two hanging around. When dealing with a space such as this with so many different variables when it comes to who is haunting the space, it could be anything from deceased humans to inhuman presences that are attracted to the dynamics. My job would be to communicate with the ghosts of the Tenth and find out what their purpose is. But the real question was ... are they here for good or evil? And that was a question I could not honestly answer at the time, so I was entering the investigation nearly blind.

But ... I had found the training ground for my team.

Two

COMING FORWARD

About a month after the staged reading, I would find myself at the Tenth once more to watch an original production by a local theater company that featured a friend of mine in the starring role. As I entered the theater, I wondered if the actors or the production team were having any weird experiences. It was like walking into a secret that everyone knew but didn't dare to speak about. Every time I walked into the building, I had a tendency to look around like a madwoman. Looking back, I probably looked foolish in trying to catch a glimpse of a ghost. But I was expecting them to make themselves known in some way so they could say hi because I was developing a relationship with the ghosts in the building.

An Actor's Experience

At this point, it was no secret that I was involved in the paranormal. I took my seat in the audience and watched a wonderful story take place on the stage. I wasn't even thinking about ghosts. At intermission, I glanced over to the curtain and was startled to see the outline of a person lingering there. It was a stationary shadow, like someone just standing to the side watching the show. Then I watched the aisle on the left side fill with people as they got up to stretch their legs. As the play ended, I stood up to give the company a standing ovation, and I hung out afterward to congratulate my friends John and Frank. In the lobby, we enjoyed hors d'oeurves and champagne. Throughout the evening, I noticed that John looked like he had something on his mind. I gave him a look that said, "Do we need to talk?" Taking it as his cue to approach me, John pulled me aside.

"So you're still into the whole ghost thing, right?" he asked.

"Yes ... ," I hesitantly answered.

John looked over to the side and gestured with his head telling me to follow him outside into the alleyway between the theater and the lofts next door. It was a cold evening in January, and I held my jacket together tightly as John buttoned up his leather jacket and tied his scarf around his neck. He was planning on being out there a while. He took one more look around to see if anyone was around or if there was a chance that we could be overheard.

"Don't think I'm crazy but ... " he started.

I cut in. "Okay, first of all, don't start with that. You're not crazy," I assured him.

It's very common to hear people say, "Don't think I'm crazy," or "You might think I'm insane." But, you always end up hearing a good story.

John took a deep breath and continued with what he wanted to tell me. "Okay, so do you know that there are ghosts here?"

I looked at him and grinned. As that grin grew wider, I turned my head down toward the ground and pulled out my emergency pack of cigarettes. I'm not a regular smoker, but when I find myself having these kinds of interactions, especially in the form of confirmation that others have had paranormal experiences, it was time to light up.

I took a long inhale and asked him to elaborate. I was curious about what John thought. I hadn't spoken to Jeff about investigating the Tenth yet, and I kept my interest in the building fairly secret because I didn't want anyone else to get involved. It wasn't even something I was ready to share among my group of friends. I tried to show my best sympathetic face, rather than the neutral demeanor I exude when clients are telling me their stories. Was I really ready to take on the Tenth Avenue Arts Center? Being that my friends were involved, it would be much harder to tell them that their experience may not have been paranormal, as opposed to breaking the news to a complete stranger. Amazing how feelings and relationships could change the way you approach an area that you're so familiar with.

John went on to explain that during the tech week, which took place several days before his show opened, the lights would flicker with any reference to "immoral things" such as sex or sexually transmitted diseases. I looked at him with confusion, and I initially thought that the story was weird and downright silly. But apparently the occurrence happened often enough for most people to notice, and the company of actors would deliberately yell out random words such as "herpes," and the lights would flicker. Given that the content of the play wasn't very Christian, the lights flickered often.

"It sounds like you guys need to check the electrical connections on your lights," I said.

"That's the thing…we did. Everything was fine and there was no reason for the lights to flicker," he said.

I know John well enough to know that he wouldn't make this up. He was just as confused as I was. I remembered how I seemed to have had supernatural help with the lighting situation for my staged reading as well as often feeling that there was a presence up in the booth. I wondered if there might be more to John's story than the lights flickering every time someone said "herpes." If the website was correct and the space was really haunted by the Pastor, or even if there was a presence of someone who deemed themselves more religious and moral than present-day society, then maybe they were commenting on the content of the production I had just seen. Granted, this was a stretch. But this also shed some light on whether the ghosts of the Tenth had an opinion about the material being produced in the former chapel.

John wouldn't be the only actor to approach me with a personal paranormal experience. Perhaps it was a good thing that I was becoming more open with my interest in the unknown, because members of the theater community now had someone to go to when it came to sharing their experiences without judgment.

The Director's Order

Shortly after that incident, a director friend of mine, who I'll call Nicole for the purpose of maintaining her privacy, reached out to me. She wanted to meet for a long lunch and talk to me about "discreet matters about the Tenth."

Immediately upon reading her e-mail, I knew exactly what Nicole was talking about.

As I arrived at the restaurant, Nicole and I did the girly squeal and hugged. Nicole spent some time in Chicago doing some work as an actress and taking a course on directing with a professional theater company. When she returned to San Diego, she was taken on as the artistic director for a budding theater company, and I was so happy for her. We spent our college days doing summer theater in the Inland Valleys and quickly became good friends. I always knew Nicole as someone who was calm and had everything together in both her professional and private life. This was one of the first times I had a chance to have a good, long conversation with Nicole since she returned.

After catching up on what the past year brought to us and hearing Nicole reminisce about her time in Chicago, we finally got down to the purpose of our visit.

I asked her if I could take notes, and she agreed. Nicole started with telling me about how she had been spending a lot of time at the Tenth. She made it a point to note that she hadn't told this to anyone and made me promise to keep it secret. She mentioned that she had to spend a lot of time in the theater by herself with no one else in the building.

"What did you hear?" I asked.

"It isn't what I heard. It was what I saw," she said.

Nicole began to tell me about the day she found herself at the Tenth completely by herself for the first show she directed in town, but she also doubled as the lighting designer because of the company's small budget. Nicole took a day off from her regular job to spend the entire day at the Tenth. Jeff had let her in that morning and left her alone in the theater. None of the office tenants were in that day, which wasn't unusual since most of them were owned by theater companies as well, and in reality, the workday doesn't really begin until the late afternoon.

Nicole got out all of the lights that she needed for the show, and got the ladder out and set up so that she could start hanging lights on the main stage. As she made her way up the ladder, standing about twenty feet off the ground, she heard the double doors to the main stage open.

"Hello?" she asked.

There was nothing. Just her and the outside noises from the busy city.

Nicole went back to setting her lights. As she tightened the bolts one by one, light by light, she heard a loud sound.

"Get down!"

At this point, Nicole started to tear up. She was so shaken by the voice that she almost fell off the ladder. Nicole gripped the ladder so tightly that her knuckles were white. She initially thought that someone from the outside had yelled.

"Where do you think the voice came from?" I asked.

"I don't know. I thought it was coming from below me. Like Jeff had come in and wanted me to come down for my own safety. But when I looked, there was no one there. It made no sense," she said.

I told Nicole to continue, telling me as many details as she could remember.

After Nicole calmed down from the incident with the voice, she finished hanging her remaining lights and went up the stairs to the light booth so that she could turn down and focus the house lights. She was on her way back up the ladder and as she began to work on the light ... the giggle of a little girl echoed in the lobby.

"I was freaked out. I went down the ladder, grabbed my purse, and left. I was done," she said.

I sat there, marinating in the story she told me.

Then I decided to open up to her. I mentioned that I heard the giggle too. At that moment, Nicole looked at me with such relief that I thought she was going to pass out. She leaned back and put her hand to her eyes, wiping tears.

"I'm sorry. I know I'm being stupid and dramatic. But I've been replaying that moment over and over in my head. And I honestly thought I was crazy. I thought that I would get sent to the loony bin if I ever told anyone about it. I don't even want to be in the Tenth anymore unless someone is with me. I love the space; I love working with Jeff. I felt so bad about even considering breaking my relationship with the Tenth because of something like this," she said.

"Are you going to go back anytime soon?" I asked.

"Eventually," she whispered.

I then told her about my own experience at the Tenth, and reiterated the stories to her from the Tenth's website. I wanted to curb her fears to the best of my ability by telling her that while I can't confirm that what she experienced was indeed paranormal, I could give her some advice on how to cope with the experience.

"Well, here's what I can do. I can tell you that the voice that you heard in the theater probably belonged to the British Lieutenant," I began.

I told her that it was probably the British Lieutenant mentioned on the website, because the voice she had heard was commanding, almost like the person was comfortable giving orders or held a position of power. And given that the other ghosts in the building weren't known to frequent the main stage, it made the most sense in terms of whose territory she was in. In terms of the giggling, I long suspected that there was a child, or a young girl, in the building who seemed to have free rein of the space and could go wherever she pleased.

As Nicole and I parted ways, I realized that the haunting of the Tenth Avenue Arts Center, while it only took up one page on their website, was becoming a bigger deal each day. As more people worked in the theater, if the haunting at the Tenth was truly legitimate, then the eyewitness accounts would only increase. And this would mean that there would be more people having experiences they could not comprehend.

A Skeptic's Perspective

Nicole would not be the last person to pull me aside to talk about their experiences at the Tenth. This time, it would be a set designer, who I will name Dave.

At this point, the team still hadn't investigated the space. It seemed that every time I forgot to talk to Jeff about it, the theater found a way to remind me to get this important task done.

Dave was probably one of the most sought-after set designers in the city, and he also prided himself on practically building his set almost by himself. He leaves his own signature in every set he designs. Dave has also spent many hours alone in various theaters not just around the city, but also around the country. If there was anyone to talk to about weird things going on in theaters, it was Dave.

I think my conversations with John and Nicole were starting to make their way around the San Diego theater circuit because I would often get asked about the latest ghost story or investigation that I was working on while I was seeing shows or in dance classes. Everyone I encountered remained respectful and approached me with genuine curiosity. I was very blessed that the encounters went in that direction as opposed to me getting laughed at or being looked at like I was weird. I can't talk about what was said about me behind closed doors, because I wasn't there. But the fact that my "hobby" was being spoken about made people more comfortable approaching me to talk about their own experiences. There was a movement beginning in the San Diego theater community. Theater and the paranormal began to get press coverage during the Halloween season, and other theaters began to come forward with stories that their venues were haunted. People were beginning to open up, not just because of me, but from a collective effort by the community of actors and artists.

I actually ran into Dave during a rehearsal for another show I was working on, as he was also designing the set for our show along with the show he was working on at the Tenth. Dave pulled me aside and said that he has heard through the grapevine that I was the "ghost girl" now and that he had something to speak to me about. Dave was often direct to the point of being uncomfortable. I asked him to tell me what was going on.

"Here's the thing. I've been working on my set at the Tenth…"

"Oh boy," I interrupted.

"I know I'm not the first person to talk to you about this place. But it's creepy. I've been working on my set for the last few days, and I had some volunteers helping me build."

"How many?" I asked.

"At the time I got the crap scared out of me? Two. I was attaching two flats together. I was the only one on the backstage side while my two helpers were on the other side. I asked them to go outside and bring in more flats and some supplies, causing me to be by myself in the main stage area. I was looking back to admire my work when I saw the curtains move on my right, which would be house left," he said. Immediately, my mind was reminded of that time when I felt the fingers dig underneath my shoulder as I leaned against the curtain before my staged reading.

Turns out, Dave figured the curtains were a draft, so he went back to his work. Then he felt and heard someone knock on the set. He thought it was one of the volunteers being silly, so he went to the other side to tell them to get back to work and no one was there.

I looked at him with big eyes and asked him how the experience made him feel.

"Honestly? It scared the crap out of me. But I had to keep going like nothing happened," he said.

I told Dave that based on what I knew about the space, there was no need to feel threatened, and like I told Nicole, there was something there that probably wanted to communicate with him. I knew Dave could handle the talk of logical explanations, and he was already well versed in that area. As I spoke to him and let him know that he shouldn't be afraid of what he experienced, he relaxed a bit.

"So what do I do if it happens again?" he asked.

I was initially taken aback by the question. I hadn't been asked by anyone who shared stories with me on what to do should an experience happen again.

I told Dave that if he didn't wish to interact with the ghosts in the building, then to ignore it and proceed with life as usual.

"What if that does not stop it and they get more aggressive?" Dave was persistent. I told him that if ignoring it doesn't work, then there was always the option of being upfront with the ghosts and just telling them that you aren't interested in interacting, and then proceed with business as usual.

I said goodbye to Dave and went back to my rehearsal. As the evening came to a close, I couldn't think of anything else except the Tenth. There, I decided that I would start the process of exploring the Tenth as a haunted location. It was time to take off the actor hat and to get out the investigation equipment, call up the team, and tell them that we have a case on our hands. In the end, I wasn't there when John, Nicole, or Dave had their experiences. I couldn't confirm that what they had experienced was paranormal. But given what I knew about these people, and knowing that they err on the side of caution and very rarely jump to dramatic conclusions, I knew that their experiences could be true.

In the midst of these personal conversations, I kept forgetting to ask my friends if they had shared their stories with Jeff. I was inclined to think not, due to them not wanting to seem foolish. Bringing up paranormal experiences to a stranger is a brave thing to do because it exposes various vulnerabilities.

I also couldn't approach this case in the same way that I would begin working on a client case. When APS gets a new case, we rarely know the people we are working with. But in the case of the Tenth, I knew many of the people who had experiences, and it was a space that I was very familiar with—especially the main stage area. I had not gotten a chance to explore the building in detail, nor could I find my way around the Tenth comfortably. I knew that the Tenth would be a learning experience for me. I didn't even know that much about the Tenth in terms of history or Jeff's relationship with the building besides just being the owner. I wanted to know more about the Tenth and see what was haunting the building. Were the stories on the Tenth's website true? Or was there something more going on beyond what could be found on a web page?

The Pursuit

I pitched the idea more aggressively with Jeff about investigating the Tenth, and he responded with enthusiasm. If I wanted the team to go in and investigate, the building was ours to do so. All I could think was, what an incredible opportunity for any paranormal investigator!

When I told my team about the Tenth Avenue Arts Center, they were eager to check the place out. I told them to refrain from doing heavy research for the time being, since I didn't want their experiences to be influenced or "tainted" with the expectation of having interactions with only certain ghosts whose identities have been confirmed. In reality, none of the ghosts have had their identity confirmed as far as I know. The team had already performed a few cases, which ended with success. I had no doubt that they could handle the Tenth Avenue case. I found a renewed excitement as I started to prepare for the investigation and getting a date secured with Jeff. I could tell that he was also excited about the opportunity to finally have a paranormal investigation team working on the case. Jeff told me his future goals for the Tenth Avenue Arts Center as a haunted building, and I felt very fortunate to be a part of that experience and contribute to the development of the project.

Unbeknownst to me, the ghosts of the Tenth were expecting me. I am fairly certain that as soon as Jeff agreed to have us come in, the ghosts already knew about me. They already knew who I was, and they were ready for me. But was I was ready for them?

Three

FOUNDATION FOR FEAR

When I first met Jeff, which took place after several visits to the Tenth, I inquired about the ghost stories on the Tenth's website and he opened up the possibility of investigating the haunting. I was one of the first people to get into the theater as a paranormal investigator. You could call it a stroke of luck since I just happened to be at the right place at the right time with the appropriate knowledge and experience. As I read the stories online, I was intrigued and wanted to know more about their origins and if there was any validity to their existence. And most importantly: were they factual?

The Interview

With so many questions I had for Jeff, the owner of the Tenth Avenue Arts Center, I often wondered if this would turn into a complicated discussion about what was transpiring at the building and me having to calm Jeff down and logically explain some of his experiences. I was curious about Jeff's personal experiences in the Tenth and whether or not he believed in the ghosts. It seemed like a conversation that probably should have happened before my team had even stepped foot inside, but the situation unfolded the way that it was meant to. Perhaps it would be advantageous to remain cold as to what Jeff's story was. And also, in reality, Jeff remained rather tight-lipped about his personal story. I really didn't know much about him or where he came from. Come to think of it, I didn't really know much about how long the building had been an arts center and what may have been going on between the time it was a church and before it became the facility that it is today. The building itself was an enigma.

As I called Jeff, I had my questions ready, and I was considering how much the Tenth had grown in the last few years. The Tenth was becoming one of the hottest spots for production companies and event planners to book for festivals, conventions, and, of course, theater performances. I was thrilled that Jeff was having so much success with the Tenth that didn't depend on any sort of paranormal projects. I had always been impressed with the way Jeff built the reputation of the Tenth by renting the building at an inexpensive price, which made it available to numerous companies that wanted a quality space to present their productions. Basically, because of this wonderful option, the theater companies could break even and make a profit more easily, and the Tenth would still make money and get exposure. The paranormal aspect didn't deter anyone from working with Jeff.

Jeff answered the phone with such a very cheerful voice that I thought I could actually hear him smile; he always treated you like your presence was the best thing that ever happened to him. After catching up for several minutes, I asked him how he came across the Tenth and why he decided to buy the building.

"Well, it was on the market for a really good price," he answered.

At that point, I started laughing a little because it's sort of a cliché since so many stories of haunted houses have started with a property being bought at "a really good price."

As he continued to talk, I learned that Jeff's story with the Tenth began in 1997, after buying the building from the First Baptist Church of San Diego. But it turned out that the church wasn't ready to completely move out when he purchased the Tenth, so he allowed the group to keep their pipe organ in the building until they were able to transport it. Jeff explained that it was part of the business deal, which probably helped him purchase the Tenth at the good price.

When the church was ready to take the pipe organ, Jeff was there to assist with moving the pieces down to the truck, and that was where he first learned of the stories of the ghosts:

Missy, the Pastor, and the British Lieutenant. One of the people moving the organ told Jeff the detailed stories of how Missy fell down the stairs to her death on the second floor, and in his guilt of possibly having a hand in the ending of a young life, the Pastor hung himself in the cloak room in the main stage area.

The church volunteer also told Jeff about the ghost of the British Lieutenant, who temporarily possessed his doctor, and when the doctor came to the chapel to pray for the lieutenant's soul, he made the building his home for the afterlife. The backstory behind this haunting was that a Navy doctor, who had been treating numerous patients in World War II, would often go and pray for the soldiers that he wasn't able to save. While working in a field hospital in Okinawa, one of these soldiers came from the United Kingdom and held the rank of lieutenant, and as the doctor held on to the man's heart trying to keep him alive, he felt the beating stop. At that moment, the doctor felt a very odd sensation all over his body and decided that the stresses of working in a battlefield hospital were getting to him. Feeling distraught over this particular soldier, when the lieutenant's ship came into port in San Diego, he headed over to the chapel to pray for the soul of the British man that he was unable to save. When the doctor arrived at the Tenth, he talked to the church staff about what had happened and entered the sanctuary. As he began to pray, he was pulled back into the pew and his head tilted up to the ceiling with his mouth and eyes wide open, much like the feeling and sensation that he had felt back at the hospital where he was trying to save the British Lieutenant. It was then that one of the members of the church staff found the doctor slumped over on the floor and unconscious. The doctor woke up and recovered from the incident. From then on, the British Lieutenant is said to haunt the main stage, and can often be heard giving orders in the middle of the night.

The Origin of Gossip

According to the volunteer, the source of their stories was the church's historian, who relayed the stories by word of mouth. So, Jeff was hearing about these three ghosts down the story-telling line, which probably emulated the game of telephone. But, hey, that's okay. I think what really intrigued me was the fact that a church, a Christian institution that normally doesn't humor the notion of ghosts, had stories to tell. When Jeff heard the stories, he listened, but kept them in the back of his mind.

My primary interest was the rumor of Missy's death. Given that the building was a church—and one of the most prominent churches in the San Diego area—having a child die under their watch was the perfect recipe for controversy and scandal that could have very well ruined the church, or at least harmed its reputation enough to affect membership. Of course, we also have to consider how much we know about the history of the buildings we are involved with every day, and who possibly died in them. From apartments, houses, places of work, to churches, it is information that is not readily given to the general public.

After he purchased the building and the church was completely moved out (pipe organ and all), the building sat dormant for a few years before he rented it to a few dot-com companies in 2000. Eventually those companies folded and moved out. So there were periods of time when the Tenth would sit empty with nothing going on inside. But, as Jeff stated, he bought the building at a good price, so he could afford to let it sit empty at times. Even when he rented it to tenants during this downtime, no one really asked if the space was haunted or not.

In 2007, Jeff rented the building to another church for a few months. I have to say that churches can make the best theaters. There is already a stage with a sound system, lights, and a place for the audience to sit. Churches could make a lot of money renting out their spaces to local theater companies. In that same year, Jeff gathered the assistance of Sledgehammer Theatre and Eveoke Dance Company to turn the main stage into a viable performance space. Once he realized the potential of the building as a performing arts space, Jeff began to work to renovate the bathrooms, give the building a fresh new paint job, as well as remodel and renovate the offices and box office area. This was all completed in 2008. Then in 2009, the Tenth got a new air conditioning and heating system, and the art studios were completed and available to local artists. Jeff's overall goal for the Tenth was to be an affordable hub for all local artists to come together and make art, as well as being a space for audiences and patrons to celebrate the arts scene in San Diego.

As Jeff was speaking about the renovations, I thought about how the paranormal activity seemed to have escalated in the early days of the Tenth serving as a theater, and once I got my timeline straight, I realized that was when the renovations were taking place. In the paranormal community, it has been speculated that changing the property, such as remodeling or renovating the interior, has been known to stir up paranormal activity. The theory is that the ghosts are upset with their environment changing and that they are making an attempt to put a stop to it. Another theory is that the very action of reconstructing or changing the appearance of the interior can stir up different kinds of energy. Maybe Jeff inadvertently stirred up the paranormal activity while prepping the space to become a full-fledged theater and arts center.

Making Themselves Known

The next question I asked was whether Jeff had ever had any paranormal experiences at the Tenth. I was shocked to hear that his answer was no! Besides hearing strange sounds, which he usually chalked up to pigeons and the fact that it was an old building, he didn't have any direct interactions with the ghosts at the Tenth. But this wasn't the first time that the owner of a haunted location did not have any firsthand paranormal experiences. Bobby Mackey, the owner of Bobby Mackey's Music World, which skyrocketed into popularity after a mainstream ghost hunting show put their spotlight on the property for its history of gruesome murder and connections with demonic activity, also had minimal personal paranormal experiences on the site. And considering that he has owned the building since 1978 and the business is still booming, he doesn't seem to be too worried about the possible evil that could be looming.

But still, finding out that Jeff had not experienced anything significant in the building disillusioned the perfect case that I had come up with in my head. Honestly, in my mind, I had this image of Jeff continuously working on the Tenth, taking loving care of the building as the ghosts observed him from the side very cautiously, careful never to disturb. So upon learning about Jeff's lack of paranormal interactions, I started to speculate why he even bothered bringing my team in to investigate. Considering the amount of time Jeff has probably spent in the building by himself, I had expected to hear stories of him seeing a full-body apparition or having a conversation with one of the ghosts. However, looking back at the times that we spoke about the paranormal activity, Jeff called us in to confirm that the ghosts were present and not from a perspective of "Please help me deal with this."

So, I decided to just go ahead and ask Jeff the difficult question. I asked him why he was even bothering to explore this haunting when he hadn't had any personal experience.

"Well, other people were asking me if the theater was haunted, and the stories kept coming to the point where I want to see if a group of professionals could confirm it or not," he said.

Interesting.

I asked Jeff who was the first person to ask him about the building potentially being haunted, and he mentioned a tech person by the name of Jessica. She spent a lot of time by herself in the Tenth and was one of the first people who tried to establish some kind of communication with the ghosts. Jeff mentioned that she also went around the building with a plate of burning sage. He didn't quite know if she was trying to appease the ghosts of the Tenth or if she was trying to get rid of them. Sage has a long reputation for removing spirits from buildings, but there is also some controversy, as some believe that sage attracts spirits more than it repels. There have also been stories of sage awakening more spirits as well as signaling to the spirit world that the location is ready and willing to take on more ghosts. There are so many variations of sage, and given that Jessica was unreachable, Lord only knows what kind of sage she used and what her intentions were.

Based on Jeff's description of Jessica, I assumed that she wasn't around anymore. So here he was, getting questions and stories of people who had unexplainable experiences at the Tenth but with no direction on what to do about it. While Jessica probably meant well, it is possible that she contributed to escalating the activity in addition to the renovations that were taking place in the theater. This could also explain why the dot-com tenants didn't report anything weird to Jeff. There is also a stigma attached to the paranormal that still put people into hiding about their own experiences, regardless of the mainstream media making the paranormal more "normal."

I made an attempt to reach out to Jessica, and while she was open to non-paranormal-related small talk, as soon as I asked about the Tenth being haunted, she stopped responding to me.

For a moment, I had wondered whether Jeff actually believed that the theater was haunted. But I want to note that he approaches things from a very logical standpoint. He doesn't hear footsteps and assume it is paranormal; he thinks about the fact that the Tenth is an old building or that it could be rodents. Basically, he tries to debunk as much as possible. And since he couldn't confirm whether the building was haunted or not, he decided to bring in a paranormal team. Who were the people that were reporting the strange occurrences?

The people who spend a lot of time in the dark.

A Tech's Nightmare

While the Tenth was still in the early stages of becoming a venue for theaters to produce their work, there were often technicians in the field of lights and sound who spent long days and late nights at the theater. From these late nights, Jeff reported that some of the technicians were having their own experiences or watching others experience the unknown. Now, most theater people thrive in the late-night production time frame. Techies, as they're affectionately called, often work alone in the theater for long hours that go late into the night. As far as I know, there's not an onslaught of techies who are coming forward with their paranormal stories, which leads me to believe that they don't happen all that often. Of course, that leads to the disappointment that perhaps not all theaters are haunted, or their experiences are being explained by tiredness and fatigue. This also made me curious as to how much the experiences were from just the knowledge of the ghosts versus personal experience. Jeff wasn't very open about the ghost stories he had learned, but when he kept getting approached by people who seem to be having their own experiences, it was time to bring in others to investigate.

So, with the lack of personal experiences from Jeff, I asked him why he wanted to go public with the ghost stories he heard from the church member who moved the pipe organ out of the building. Jeff said that the occurrences, which were witnessed by several people, were worth investigating. He wanted to know whether the stories had the potential of having even just the sliver of truth.

For a while, Jeff only took a mental note of the experiences and continued business as usual. As I have stated numerous times, the stories must have come from somewhere. And without Jeff even mentioning anything to the tech people, he was being asked about whether the building was haunted. This also gave Jeff the idea to post the stories about the ghost on the website, seeing that there was potential. He shared with me that he wanted to one day do ghost tours around the Tenth, but wanted to first confirm that there was something weird going. I agreed with his direction.

Jeff then alerted me about something that the drop cam in the main stage picked up once on a late night. The camera is motion sensitive, and in the darkness, an orb was captured on the drop cam. Now, it is my job to remain skeptical as much as possible and debunk the evidence as it comes my way. With the drop cam video, I had to resist the urge to quickly believe what I was seeing, and because this video was captured in the middle of the night, no one was there to physically see the anomaly with the naked eye. The orb was certainly interesting and seemed to be emitting its own light. So, I couldn't debunk the video. And given the reported activity in the main stage area, it made me wonder if there was a connection that was stronger than glazing over the evidence and calling it dust. It was something to make note of and keep in my back pocket. For me to tell Jeff it was paranormal would go against the code of ethics that I made my team adhere to, but by the same token, so would telling him it wasn't anything odd. I had to declare the video as unexplainable.

As my conversation with Jeff continued, I went over our case report structure with him, which would be sent to him after each investigation along with any significant photos that were captured. I told him my personal thoughts about the haunting at the Tenth, and how I believed that the building would remain an ongoing case since it is difficult to determine a haunting, let alone analyze what kind of haunting, and the identities of the ghosts, in just one visit. Multiple visits are needed because it helps determine consistency and provides the opportunity to catch things that may have been missed from previous visits. There was no doubt that I had my work cut out for me in researching the Tenth, and I needed to dive deeper into the history of the church as well.

Four

INTO THE PAST

The old saying goes that those who don't care about history are doomed to repeat it. And the history of the Tenth lies in the three ghosts: Missy, who fell down the stairs to her death while being chased by her pastor; the Pastor himself, who committed suicide; and then we have the British Lieutenant standing guard in the main stage, caught in his loop of giving orders in the war.

So here we come to probably the most important and yet confusing chapter of the book. This is the part where I talk to you about the historical research and how everything mysteriously corroborates the haunting at the Tenth and how incredible it is. Well, we might need to rethink that. For me, this is the most frustrating part of the paranormal investigation field. While it is enlightening because you learn so much about the past and the people who lived there, it is also the number one place where you hit brick walls. Historical research can also plant seeds of doubt in the one who experienced the paranormal phenomenon or those who told the ghost stories with ignorance, not realizing that there's no data to back up their claims. Along with discussing the historical research, I'll also discuss possible theories as to why the Tenth is haunted and why people continue to have experiences.

Why Research?

Historical research is an integral part of the paranormal investigation process. The information you garner not only can validate the haunting, it can provide specific names and scenarios linked to the deceased that you can use during on-site investigations. One pioneer in the paranormal investigation field, John Sabol, has created a groundbreaking methodology that includes performing with the context of the deceased in mind and creating a hospitable environment that welcomes and encourages a conversation and response. Mr. Sabol has been able to capture compelling evidence proving that his methodology is effective.

By doing historical research, you let yourself become familiar with the space in a more intimate manner, and you're more equipped to ask productive questions that will hopefully spark a conversation between the living and the other side. Conversely, there are teams that will go into haunted locations completely blind, as they don't want to taint their experiences or produce false positives, which are real concerns. However,

I have mixed feelings about this because I feel that going in cold would result in rather unproductive conversations, which would prompt you to do the research and then return with the context. I think that in every paranormal experience, there is someone wanting to communicate. And therefore, we should do our homework so we are ready and informed to continue such communication. But sometimes, the historical research isn't readily available, or there are secrets that have been covered up for so long that they are now the product of myth and legend. The investigator's job is to unearth the secrets with the history to the best of their ability and use it in a productive manner once they begin the investigation.

To that end, I feel discussing the ghosts of the Tenth will not make much sense to readers without some background knowledge of the building, the land, and at least some history of San Diego to serve as reference points. Given that the Tenth Avenue Arts Center's history is intertwined with religion, it makes an interesting case for the spiritual presence that seems to affect the building and those who inhabit it.

Foundation of Stone

Let's start from the beginning. The Tenth was a chapel, called Draper Chapel, commissioned by a generous donor who attended the First Baptist Church of San Diego a mile or two away from where the Tenth stands. The Reverend C. F. Weston organized the first congregation on June 5, 1869, and the building was one of two churches in the "new" San Diego area by the bay. The building was erected on a lot on Seventh Street near F Street thanks to a generous donation by Alonzo Horton, who was an important figure in the development of downtown San Diego (and a Unitarian). The building was constructed in autumn, and the first worship service took place in October. Mr. Horton also gave the First Baptist Church their first bell, which was the first church bell to be used in "new" San Diego as well. Interestingly enough, the church building was dedicated on October 31, 1869, which we all know is also Halloween. Also, Reverend C. F. Weston stepped back as the leader, and was replaced by Reverend B. S. McLafferty. The church was incorporated in 1887 and then moved to a different building on the corner of Tenth Avenue and E Street in 1888 and cost about $32,000 to build. Reverend McLafferty resigned in 1873 and was replaced by O. W. Gates, who stayed for eight years. To make the breakdown simpler, here is the timeline of pastors at First Baptist Church of San Diego:

- C. F. Weston—June–December 1869

- B. S. McLafferty—August 1869–January 1873

- O. W. Gates—1873–1881

- A. J. Sturtevant—1881–1882

- Edwin C. Hamilton—1882–1883

- W. H. Stenger—1883–1885

- A. Chapman—Two months in 1885

- E. P. Smith—Two months in 1885
- W. F. Harper—1888–1893
  (New church on Tenth and E was being built)
- A. E. Knapp—1893–1900
- Walter Benwell Hinson—June 1900–1910
- W. H. Geisweit—Time unknown
- Dr. John Bunyan Smith—1925–1946
- Reverend Dr. Paul K. Whiteker—1950–1954
- Pieter Smit—1960, 1962, 1966, 1967

Multiple Locations

The first site of the church was on Seventh Street, the second and third sites both sat at the corner of Tenth and E, and the fourth (and current) site sits in an area called University City, which is about fifteen to twenty minutes away from downtown on a street called Governor Drive. What is interesting about the second site of the church was that it was torn down and rebuilt twice.

This is a postcard from the First Baptist Church of San Diego.
The caption on the back, in part, reads: "Dr. John Bunyan Smith, Pastor.
Oldest Protestant Church in San Diego. Organized in 1869. Present
Membership: 4,500. Church plant consists of 84 rooms, auditorium
seating 1,600, and beautiful Draper Chapel. Location 10th and E, San
Diego, CA." The X on the photo marks the portion of the building that is
currently the Tenth Avenue Theater. Courtesy of Jeff Cotta.

The second site of the Church on Tenth and E that is next door to the Tenth has now become renovated lofts for rent. The first building on that site was erected in 1888 and then it was torn down and rebuilt into what is now called "The White Temple" in 1966. As stated before, the Tenth Avenue Arts Center was first built as a chapel, commissioned by a generous donor. The donor's idea behind it was that since San Diego was a port where sailors and other military people were arriving at all times throughout the day and night, there should be a place of worship where these men could go to at anytime to pray for their friends, family, and comrades. The chapel construction began in 1928 and was completed in 1930. Not only did the chapel serve as a twenty-four-hour venue for military, it also hosted youth and other events for the church as well as Boy Scout meetings. The chapel was a multipurpose building. Who knew if this donor or the builders would ever know what they created?

Lining It Up

The origins of the Tenth building line up with the ghost story of the British Lieutenant. If he did indeed attach himself to the doctor who treated him, then he had a one-way ticket to the Tenth. The doctor probably took advantage of the church's twenty-four-hour chapel to pray for the soldiers that he wasn't able to save. When he recounted his story from Okinawa to the church staff, it likely awakened the spirit of the British Lieutenant, who then realized that he found the place where he wanted to rest for eternity. After the Lieutenant left his body, the doctor was able to wake up and walk away from the building. But the soldier remained.

Looking at this from a distance, a believer in the paranormal can hypothesize that perhaps the British Lieutenant now found a spiritual place where he could reside during the afterlife. As discussed in the previous chapter, these were stories that Jeff was told as he was helping the church volunteer move the pipe organ down the stairs. We should also consider the fact that the British Lieutenant could be residual energy that was left behind after the doctor prayed for his soul. Since the city of San Diego is a military-rich town, there are constant triggers occurring on a regular basis, which may inspire the British Lieutenant to give them orders on what they should be doing. Given that the church most likely hosted numerous military men in the chapel, and several probably did pass out from exhaustion, it would be curious to see if this doctor's story actually made the papers. But in the most likely case, when the doctor retold his story to the staff member, it remained on the ears and then retold, never to be written down.

When Jeff had a medium come to the building, she stated that she felt the presence of a man who had served in the military outside of the United States, and she was confused over why he would be in the Tenth and not someplace closer to home.

A Life Cut Short

The next ghost up for discussion is Missy. As probably the most interesting and yet controversial ghost haunting the Tenth, she quickly became my primary focus. The intrigue is mainly due to the lack of information on her beyond what is on the Tenth's website. Missy's story goes like this: She was with her youth group having a gathering on the roof, which was used for recreational activities such as badminton, basketball, and volleyball. This was all taking place in October, and the fall season in San Diego is relatively mild but sometimes can be a bit hot. This particular day was scorching, and Missy didn't want to stick around outside. The Pastor who was supervising the activities told her that once the current basketball game was completed, everyone would head downstairs to enjoy refreshments in the second-floor social hall. Missy didn't want to wait any longer than she had to, so she headed inside unsupervised. When the Pastor saw this, he handed the game off to one of the older kids and told the kids what to do after the game was over, and then bolted after Missy, who had already gone down the first flight of stairs by herself. Because of my experience working in education with children from age two through eleven, I found myself relating to the Pastor, as children will sometimes do as they please or, to put it in a nice way, dance to the beat of their own drum.

Once she realized that the Pastor was following her when he called out her name, Missy decided to make a game out of it and yelled, "Catch me if you can!" while gaining speed down the stairs with the Pastor in pursuit. As he reached the landing between the third and second floor, he heard Missy shout, "Catch me..." before hearing a scream and several thumps. Frightened over what may have happened, the Pastor kept going.

Missy was found dead at the bottom of the stairs on the second floor; her head was split open and blood pooled under her body. As the Pastor gazed upon the girl's crumpled body, his life changed forever, as he became burdened with the extreme guilt that he may have caused Missy's death. There is no doubt that Missy's death stopped the entire building and maybe even the entire block. Activities were put on hold, Missy's family was notified, and the grieving process sprung into action. It is also likely that the Pastor who was going after Missy down the stairs was the same one presiding over her funeral, which likely took place in the church next door if her parents were active members. The death of a child is always tragic, especially in the event of an accident. Unfortunately, death takes on a starring role in our society, and can sneak up on us when we least expect it. In the case of Missy's death, based on the information that I have, no one was at fault; it was just an unfortunate turn of events.

So, with this in mind, the first question I had was whether Missy was real or not. Or perhaps "Missy" was a nickname or another name used as a cover up to protect identities. Before completely analyzing the topic of Missy, one needs to look into the story of the Pastor after Missy's death.

This is the stairwell where Missy died. Her body was found on the landing.
Courtesy of Jeff Cotta.

This is the same stairwell from a different angle. Courtesy of Jeff Cotta.

Burdened with Guilt

The story goes on to say that the Pastor never did quite recover from Missy's death and lived with the burden of guilt on a daily basis. He lived with the "what if?" questions. What would have happened if he didn't run the stairs, but instead, simply walked down to meet Missy? Would she still have interpreted the action as a game? Or would she have just gone about her business and met the Pastor at the bottom of the stairs? The Pastor couldn't make peace or accept what had happened, and Missy's final words of "Catch me…" continued to haunt him. Eventually, the two words would transition from words from a game to words of a desperate plea to catch her before she fell to her death.

The next part of the story from the Tenth's website actually gives a specific date: November 25, 1963, just three days after the assassination of John F. Kennedy. The Pastor reportedly had given a very inspirational speech about being strong during one of the nation's toughest times, which affected many members of the church, including the secretary. The next day, which was Monday, the secretary entered the building, ready to perform her administrative duties for the day. She knocked on the Pastor's door to his second-floor office, but received no answer. She walked back down to the first floor and went to the sanctuary and continued to call out the Pastor's name. Still no answer. The cloakroom, which was on the right side of the altar and housed the choir robes, emitted a faint light. Thinking that the Pastor was cleaning up the robes and room after the service on Sunday, the secretary continued to walk down the aisle, calling out the Pastor's name. Once she entered the cloakroom, she looked up and screamed in horror as she saw the Pastor's body hanging from the storage loft. The Pastor had committed suicide.

Let's go back now to analyzing Missy. Upon initial search through historical records, there isn't much evidence to support that there was a death in the church. However, given that it was the early to mid-sixties when this incident likely took place, it may be safe to hypothesize that perhaps the church didn't want the information out there. If you look at it from a perspective of preserving a reputation, it would have looked really bad for the church that they had a child die under their watch. Given that the First Baptist Church of San Diego was one of the largest Baptist churches in the area, Missy's death could have easily stirred up controversy. But it is unlikely that such a sensational story would have been swept under the rug unless Missy's parents were talked into keeping it quiet, leaving Missy's manner of death to become a legend that was whispered among fellow church members, but never confirmed. If this is the case, I would find that to be on the brink of being disrespectful to her memory as well as the memory of the Pastor.

There is one girl who passed away in San Diego around the ideal time frame of Missy's death, she was born in 1955, and died in 1966. But her name wasn't Missy. During her regular "sightings," she is seen wearing a green and white striped dress with a green headband, and is described on the website as having mid-length dark hair and bangs that went straight across her forehead. Here we have a problem. The girl died three years after the Kennedy assassination, and the Pastor was noted to have committed suicide just days after the national tragedy. It is not very likely that the girl I found is the Missy that we are looking for, if we assume the dates given are true. Here we find ourselves with possible scenarios, but because there is lack of historical evidence to strongly support these stories, there can't be any confirmation. Perhaps Missy and the Pastor are an accumulation of several events that occurred behind the walls of the chapel.

Now, who was the Pastor who committed suicide from the guilt of causing Missy's death? This is another mystery. To date, none of the head pastors at the First Baptist Church of San Diego committed suicide. But given the size of the church at that time, with several hundred members, it might be possible that the suicidal pastor was an assistant pastor or maybe a youth pastor. Matching up historical records with the information on the Tenth's website, Pastor Pieter Smit was the head pastor at the time of John F. Kennedy's assassination, and it does line up with the fact that he did give an inspirational speech over the tragedy. Truthfully, Smit was a very well-known Baptist pastor who led many people in the Christian faith and garnered his own little rise to fame with his inspirational speech. But he didn't kill himself a few days later. He actually lived to the ripe old age of ninety-four. News of a pastor committing suicide would probably have made headlines at least around the county. But again, given the circumstances and the reputation of the First Baptist Church of San Diego, it may be possible that the suicide was swept under the rug.

Lack of Evidence

Granted, the recordkeeping back in the mid-twentieth century was not nearly as tight as it is today with the modern age of the Internet. Word of mouth and newspapers delivered mainstream news back in that day. Death records were all paper until just a few decades ago when they went digital. Records are still being updated as we speak and uploaded onto the Internet for public viewing. So, perhaps there is still a chance that we might find something that will fill in the missing link when it comes to Missy and the Baptist pastor. There are three men who have been found to be pastors at First Baptist Church of San Diego between 1940–1970; John Bunyan Smith (who lived to the age of eighty-five), Pieter Smit (who reportedly lived to be ninety-four), and Paul K. Whiteker (who lived to be eighty-five). Perhaps the story of the Pastor who committed suicide really is nothing but legend. But a part of me refuses to believe that. All stories come from somewhere, and legends tend to hold a little bit of truth. What could have happened at the church that spawned such a tragic story as this? Maybe the world will never know.

So, it seems that all we have to go by are the verbal stories that were told to Jeff. Does this mean that the Tenth Avenue Arts Center isn't haunted? Certainly not. It just means that besides digging deeper into the research aspect, we also need to start hypothesizing on theories. Which came first: the incidents or the haunting?

Let's say for a moment that the haunting came first. Let's say that the people around the chapel, as well as the kids who used the building for their recreational activities, had noticed something weird was going on but had no way to explain it. With the combination of personal stories, they may have eventually melded together into unconfirmed origin stories as an attempt to explain the weird occurrences in the chapel. If we go along with the theory that ghosts are not stationary, perhaps there is the possibility that the presences who have been interpreted as Missy, the Pastor, and the British Lieutenant are really different people who have been given these new personas.

Another factor that we need to consider is looking into the land. Before the church or the chapel were built, in fact, before San Diego was even a glimmer in the eye of its founders, the city was a hilly valley next to the bay that was home to the Kumeyaay tribe. San Diego is heralded as the birthplace of California, and it was the European settlers who first hit the shores in 1542 and claimed as land for Spain. Not too long after that, a small civilization was set up, complete with religion, that nearly wiped out the Kumeyaay people with disease and war. With this in mind, the city of San Diego was not the original location for downtown San Diego. Just several miles up north off of Interstate 5 is Old Town, which was the location of downtown San Diego until the 1860s, when

Alonzo Horton came into town and began developing a new downtown by the water, then known as "New Town." Old Town was quickly abandoned by businesses and companies who wanted to be part of the growth of the new city and be near the shipping ports. Based on the dates given, the First Baptist Church of San Diego was one of the first churches in the city, and it was able to grow as much as it did thanks to the generosity of Horton, who was also able to connect San Diego to the numerous railroads that were growing around the country. Of course, this history of "America's Finest City" is much more extensive, as I'm only including the bits of history that are relevant to the history of the Tenth.

Given the tensions with the Kumeyaay people and the richness in religious history for the area of San Diego, it can be safe to assume that it was a spiritual city. Like many older towns in the mid-nineteenth century, religion ruled and oppression was a way of life. In fact, we would not have the Tenth Avenue Arts Center in the first place if it weren't for Christianity and its Baptist connection. Now, given that the building is a spiritual place of worship, who knows what exactly could be going on supernaturally and what kind of spirits and entities are attracted to this particular building.

The Search for Validation

However, the historical research has so far left us at a dead end when it comes to validating the existence of the three ghosts. Perhaps this is the wrong way to think of things. What if the ghosts actually came first? Or what if the events that were told to Jeff really happened, but because of their controversial matter, were simply hidden away? The First Baptist Church of San Diego had well over a few thousand members, and was one of the most prominent Baptist churches in the growing city. Because of the church's silence on even something as simple as confirming the list of pastors who have presided over the congregation, the only thing we really have at this point is speculation.

So, with the lack of historical research support, is it time to hang up the ghost stories at the Tenth and consider it a bust? The answer is no. If anything, it is time to warrant more investigation from different people, who will all come together and compare notes. Perhaps it is time to be a bit more aggressive when it comes to obtaining the historical information. A lot of the issues that are encountered while researching the Tenth are the result of the church's silence. Of course, that is their right. But at the same time, if there was no credibility to the death of Missy or the suicide of the Pastor, then why don't they say so when questioned? If it is untrue, then sharing that information should not be a problem—and it could put to bed the ghosts of Missy and the Pastor. And if anything, why would a church voluntarily share the information with Jeff, a complete stranger?

Realizing that there wasn't going to be much help in the research area, it was time to reassess and approach the haunting at the Tenth with a unique perspective. The team and I would be basically going in completely blind, not knowing who we were going to be talking to and what was inhabiting the building. Did the ghosts at the Tenth even have a historic connection with the building? What if they were ghosts who were passing through and liked the space well enough to make it their permanent home? There are numerous theories to explore, and getting into the building to investigate was the next step.

Five

FIRST CONTACT

It was the night that I had been waiting for ... it was the night that I was able to bring in my team for the paranormal investigation of the Tenth Avenue Arts Center. I honestly didn't know what to expect. Besides having the short experiences while I was at the theater for other engagements, I was never really able to be in the space and focus on investigating. But here was my chance. I had three of my team members on hand: Jay, Beverly, and Rick. So, in total, four team members. Given how large the building was, we knew we were in for a long night.

But I wasn't at the theater yet. I was running late. I texted Jay to let him know who to talk to and what Jeff looked like so that they could get the key. I also called and texted Jeff to let him know who to look for and passed on Jay's contact information. By the time I arrived, Jeff was already gone.

The Team

Jay, Beverly, and Rick were in the lobby waiting for me. Jay was one of the first members to join the team, along with his wife Beverly, who was sensitive to energies around her. She could feel the feelings of the ghosts, all the while not considering herself to be psychic. Beverly considered herself to be empathic and could gather information from reading emotions. She could gather information such as gender and feelings. She and Jay had worked on a few cases before the first investigation at the Tenth. But because of scheduling conflicts, Rick hadn't yet been able to join us, so the Tenth was his first official investigation. By looking at him, I could tell he was nervous.

This wasn't their first time at the Tenth; Jay was a part of the staged reading of my play and Rick had been in attendance a few months ago. From their earlier visits, the team knew that the building was haunted even before I mentioned anything. And by this point, Jay was becoming my second-in-command.

"Did you guys get in okay?" I asked.

"Yeah, Jeff opened up the doors, showed us some hotspots to pay attention to, and left us the key," Jay replied.

"What?"

"Yep, we have the key," Jay was trying to hold back a smile that looked like he was a kid getting free candy in the candy shop. I was a bit surprised that Jeff trusted my team enough to let them hang on to the key. But he had left me the key when I did my staged reading, so I suppose that it wasn't that much of a surprise. But still, we were left inside the Tenth unsupervised and with the key. It was a lot of trust and responsibility, and I definitely didn't want to mess it up. It was also a dream for an investigator to be left alone in a building with six floors of haunted rooms at my disposal.

"Since you got the tour, Jay, how about we go set up tech and we'll follow your lead."

"Jeff really wants us to go to this room that he calls the 'writing room,'" Jay suggested.

As we walked, I realized that I almost forgot something very important.

"Make sure you turn on your recording devices… just for the hell of it," I said. While I knew we needed to have our recording devices on for the entire investigation, we had just gotten started with our setup and were in the midst of walking up the stairs to our destination.

"Every room seems to have its own energy," Beverly commented as we walked up the flight of stairs and passed the rooms. I asked her what that meant, and she said that each room had a different feeling and emotion associated with it. None of the rooms had a uniform energy. It could have been due to anything from the office tenants having their own energy to the ghosts who frequented the rooms they were the most comfortable with. She was right. Each room in the building had its own energy and personality. It felt as if we were walking on the sidewalk of a neighborhood. But instead of walking on a sidewalk, we were walking up flights of stairs and down the halls. And instead of houses, we were walking by rooms. It made me wonder if each room was occupied by a different ghost, and they were watching us from the windows wondering what we were doing there. Beverly could tell if the inhabitant of the room was a female or male, and if they were happy in their current situation.

The Writing Room

We headed to the third floor, where Jay unlocked the door and opened it to a room with a large table with chairs all around. There was also a mirror in the room. Immediately I was met with a cold breeze. There were windows, but none of them were open. I also took note of the outside noise that we heard in the room. I hadn't realized how loud it could potentially be in the Tenth, but I made sure my team members tagged everything, even if it seemed small. "Tagging" on a paranormal investigation means that while we are recording audio, if a dog barked outside, we would briefly mention the sound, or "tag" it so to speak, so we knew it wasn't paranormal when we did our evidence review. Because sure enough, we would forget what happened and mistake it as paranormal phenomenon.

Because we were limited on space, I told everyone that we would sit in the chairs around the table. As a team, we conducted a short meditation and prayer for protection and for a productive investigation, and we began with our session of asking questions and hoping to get a response in the form of electronic voice phenomenon (EVP for short).

"Hello, my name is Alex. And this is Jay, Beverly, and Rick," I started.

I had the rest of the team introduce themselves, and I told them to feel free to ask questions and that I didn't want to be the only one making conversation with the unseen presences. We were met with silence. That didn't alarm me or surprise me since sometimes there could be replies that we can't hear with our naked ears that come up as recorded EVPs. As we began to ask questions about the names of the people who were in the building and why the ghosts were there at the theater, we began to hear heavy footsteps above us.

"What is that?" Rick asked.

"Are you kidding me?" I asked with disbelief.

How cliché was that? Heavy footsteps on the floor above us. I knew that no one else was in the building, and the floors and ceilings were made of cement. Of course, there were pipes and such in between the flooring, and it might have been rodents. But these were very distinct steps as if someone was walking slowly across the floor.

I decided to get out my candle. I saw there was a tall mirror directly across the room from me, and I had been practicing scrying at home and wanted to see if I could establish some sort of communication. As I placed myself in front of the mirror holding my candle, I felt uneasy and hesitated to focus on the area behind me. I said a prayer, opened my circle, and started talking. I told the ghosts about myself and how I came to the theater often.

A lot of activity has taken place in the writing room.
Courtesy of Jeff Cotta.

The practice of scrying, which dates back thousands of years, started out as looking for images and visions in water. It was commonly used in the military as a method to try to spy on enemies and gather information. History has shown that ancient civilizations such as Persia and Greece practiced scrying, and the practice even has Celtic origins. It involves looking into some sort of translucent object such as water, crystal, or in my case, a mirror. While not proven, investigators and researchers alike have claimed to have seen the deceased in their reflection or see images that are communicated from the unseen presence as a message. There are different ways to scry with mirrors. The most common is to sit in a dark room with a candle. But there have also been mirrors specifically made for scrying that have been painted black.

"Do you enjoy the performances that take place here?" I asked.

The Fourth-Floor Theater

I wasn't feeling much when it came to a response. It was almost as if the presence in the room was either uninterested in what I had to say, didn't realize I was talking, or had left the room. It was an odd feeling. The cold breeze was gone, and there was an empty feeling in the room. I closed my circle, said another prayer, and blew out the candle.

"Should we go ahead and head to the fourth floor?" Jay asked.

"Yeah, we're not getting much more in the writing room," I replied.

We packed up what we brought out, Jay locked the door, and we started the journey up another flight of stairs. So as the team went up the stairs to the next floor, I made some general observations about the space and our surroundings. The lights kicked on as we walked up each floor.

"Automatic lights... good to know." You never know what could happen with lights that could kick on from a motion detector or what could ensue with lights that turn off by themselves. We noted this to curb against false positives with our data collection. I started to turn off the automatic sensors so we could be in the building in complete darkness. Immediately, the team started getting apprehensive and tense. There was no doubt that the Tenth had a legitimately creepy vibe in the dark, being that it was an old building and things echoed. And given that we were in the building by ourselves, it was easy to freak out at every little thing. Finally, Jay opened the door to what would be our headquarters for the evening.

We entered a large horizontal room that Jeff wanted to turn into a small theater. There was a crew filming something in that room, so I made a mental note to not touch anything. The set looked a lot like a scene from *Alice in Wonderland* with the small table covered in teacups, as well as flowers, chairs, and costumes that looked like they belonged to the Mad Hatter. Seeing the mannequin in the corner didn't make it any less creepy. There was a power strip to the left of us, which was where I set up my laptop and we plugged in our computers. On the other side of the room over by the window was a small stage and little backstage area. The entire group admitted to getting some uneasy feelings in that area, and we decided to save it for later.

"Okay, so we're going to split up," I announced.

Immediately I was met with big eyes. My team members were still very much new to investigating, and this was Rick's first investigation with the team. I didn't think there would be a lot going on at the Tenth initially because my paranormal experiences were very minimal. But still, I planned to pair Rick up with a more experienced team member such as myself or Jay, since they were friends and worked together. They clearly had a good working relationship and Jay could talk Rick through stressful situations.

"It's really cold in here," Rick commented.

"Yeah, it's a bit chilly," I quickly replied. I hadn't let the temperature really bug me because I was wearing a jacket and it wouldn't be a surprise that this room was drafty. And if my team members were showing any signs of anxiety like Rick was, I wanted to counter it with a calm demeanor and confidence in order to try to ease the anxiety and tension. I wanted to make it clear that the temperature wasn't a big deal and not something to focus on at the moment.

"So what we're going to do is that two of you are going to stay in here and partake in the Ganzfeld experiment while the other two are two floors up checking out the space and doing an EVP session on the roof," I said.

The Ganzfeld experiment is a sensory-deprivation experiment that is basically used to test out psychic abilities. There
is a sender and a receiver. The receiver wears white glasses
(or ping-pong balls) while wearing headphones that give off
white noise and looking into a red light. The idea behind it is
that taking away your normal senses will heighten your psychic senses and enhance your ability to pick up information
from the sender. Typically, the sender could be psychically
sending a word, a photo, or an action. Interestingly enough, it
has been said that artistic people have better results with the
Ganzfeld than people who aren't involved in the arts or some
form of creativity. So what was the point of using it in a paranormal investigation? Well, think of the ghost, the survival of
the living's consciousness, as the sender, and us—the living—
acting as the receiver. Results can be debatable, but it's still
interesting when there are hits in the sender/receiver activity.

As we were setting up, Jay made note of the piano while
Rick began to play it.

"Well, music can be a good trigger object," I stated.

At that moment, Rick stopped playing. I could tell he
was nervous and didn't seem to want to provoke any extra
activity. Granted, it was a fairly quiet night so far, but Rick
was so tense that I actually wondered if he was expecting
someone to jump out at him and spook him.

Jay volunteered to be the first to go under the Ganzfeld
in our HQ room. I got him set up and reminded him that
there was no back to the chair. I sent Beverly and Rick out of

the room and told them to walk the halls two floors up to the roof and get acquainted with the space. Jay also volunteered to be in the room by himself, and I got him set up for a ten-minute session.

An Unexpected Visitor

Beverly, Rick, and I decided to head up to the roof, where performances took place as well as banquets and parties. Rick shut the door behind us and latched it, which was easy to do since the wind helped blow it shut. As soon as I stepped outside, I noticed that the wind was blowing hard. As the three of us walked around, we stopped in the middle of the space, and I looked at the door. I watched the door unlatch and squeak…

The door swung open—going against the direction of the wind.

"No … way," Rick said in disbelief.

"Are you kidding me?" I said in shock.

"Did you shut the door all the way?" Beverly asked.

"Yes!" Rick replied.

"There's no way the wind could have opened that door," I said matter-of-factly.

I honestly thought Jay was behind the door because it unlatched and looked like it opened with an arm behind it.

Immediately, Beverly mentioned that maybe it really was the wind. So I reopened the door just a crack and waited for the wind to swing the door open again.

Nothing.

"I think this place is going to warrant multiple visits," I said.

The roof of the Tenth isn't immune to paranormal activity.
Courtesy of Jeff Cotta.

"I feel like something actually followed us up here," Beverly announced.

There was no doubt that the roof had a creepy feeling to it, with the howling wind, the emptiness, and the foggy San Diego skyline in our view. In situations like this, I try to remain objective and skeptical. But the incident with the door even shook me up a bit, especially since my initial attempts to debunk the situation with the door had failed.

We asked for the presence to open the door again. But we didn't get anything more besides the creepy feelings and the elevated blood pressure, so we went back down to the fourth floor where Jay was sitting and waiting for us. It was hard to believe that only ten minutes had gone by since the experience with the door, so we continued to walk down the stairs and further explore the space. For whatever reason, the entire group fell silent as we looked into the windows of the offices.

Finally, Beverly broke the silence. "I really feel like something is with us right now. Like, watching us!"

As mentioned, Beverly is sensitive and empathic, and she has been able to sense extra presences around us. I trusted her judgment while trying to not get caught up in the fright of the evening. I made an extra note every time she mentioned something about feeling an extra presence or when she was able to give specific details for the purpose of aligning it with events or anomalies that may come up during the evidence review.

As we walked back to the room where Jay was, the door was open and he looked visibly shaken up.

"Was that y'all making that big-ass noise? Slamming that door? I could feel the vibrations and everything. And I heard clear voices and someone walking around me and I heard a girl screaming," Jay said.

"When? Just now?" I asked.

"No, maybe a few minutes ago."

I decided we needed to retrace our footsteps and have Jay waiting in the room with the intention of seeing if we were, in fact, what was making the noise. With Jay back under the Ganzfeld for a few minutes, we retraced our footsteps. We went back up and closed the door, and I even did it a second time and slammed the door.

"I feel like it's mocking us. Like it's saying, 'I'm here but you don't really know,'" said Beverly. It was odd to hear her speak with such confidence in her reading. Even though her purpose wasn't to be the team psychic medium, she sounded as confident as a seasoned psychic. After we repeated our rounds a few times, we went back down to where Jay was.

"Anything?"

"Nope … that was nothing like I had experienced. I also got touched on my arm," Jay replied. "Honestly? I couldn't hear a damn thing inside this room, but I can hear everything that is going on outside. It doesn't make sense. You'd think I'd be able to better hear everything that is happening in this room right now."

We recounted our story about the door on the roof to Jay. Our investigation, which started as fun and lighthearted took a darker turn, as we didn't anticipate the experiences that had taken place so early in the process.

"Any other volunteers for the Ganzfeld?" I asked hesitantly.

"I'll do it if someone stays in the room with me," Beverly replied.

"Yeah, I guess I'll do it too. But I don't want to be by myself," said Rick.

"So who wants to go next?" I asked.

"I'll go, but you need to stay with me because I know you won't leave me," Beverly said as she glanced at Jay and Rick, who both cracked a humorous smile.

Waiting in the Corner

I sent the guys up to the roof while Beverly started her session under the Ganzfeld.

The session started quietly, but then Beverly felt something touching her and getting into her face and commented that her face was getting cold.

"I don't mind you touching me, but can you get out of my face?" she asked. After a moment, she thanked whoever she was talking to and noted that her face became warm again.

I sat quietly and observed as she continued to ask questions. Beverly continued to comment about hearing someone or something stomping around her, while I noticed that there was a dramatic drop in temperature.

"Is there a girl in this room with me?"

Thump.

This was quite a loud thump that my audio recorder was able to pick up. I didn't want to react to the sound because I didn't want to taint Beverly's experience. I wasn't exactly sure how much she could hear around her, since Jay mentioned that he couldn't hear anything inside the room while he was under the Ganzfeld. I didn't want to give her a false positive from my own noises. But I won't lie—my eyes got very big and my defenses immediately elevated. The corner near the windows and dressing rooms was getting darker and seemed to have a negative foreboding feeling.

It was at that moment I kept seeing a shadow go by the windows that looked into the hallway. I was creeped out. I really didn't know what was going on or whether my eyes were playing tricks on me.

"If you're a young girl, then why are you in the theater? Why don't you just go home?"

Rapping. And then two thumps, as if something fell on the other side of the room. I didn't know if this was a spirit trying to communicate or just a very odd coincidence. These sounds weren't occurring before Beverly's Ganzfeld session, and I wondered if the same noises had occurred while Jay was under.

"Do you want to tell me how you passed away?"

The thumps were back but sounded similar to a cart rolling over a rock. I had no idea what Beverly may have been picking up.

"My body feels tense and twisted up, like I fell down the stairs and my bones are broken. And my back was all crooked," Beverly said.

And with that, her session was over.

After I asked Beverly to retell her session experience (for consistency's sake), I made note of the taps and the thumps that happened while Beverly was under. Of course, there was the possibility that the pipes were just doing their job. Was this really happening? I was having a hard time grasping what was going on around me while Beverly was under the Ganzfeld, oblivious to the sounds around her.

"Do you keep seeing a shadow in the hallway?" Beverly asked.

At that moment, there was a pit in my stomach. I wasn't the only one who saw what was going on in the hallway.

"Yep. Funny you should mention that," I replied.

"I think it's that girl trying to get our attention."

I think Beverly was right. Missy was definitely in that hallway watching us and waiting for us to pay attention to her. Perhaps she only stayed on the outside of that room. I can't really say that I blame her. There was definitely something in the corner of the stage area that really didn't like that we were invading their space.

A Visit in Darkness

The boys returned and Jay said that he watched the door slowly close against the wind current, but nothing more. After regrouping, I decided that it was time for me to go under the Ganzfeld and see what I could experience. Rick stayed in the room with me.

My session was fairly uneventful besides feeling cold, feeling like there was something in my face, and Rick hearing clicking noises in the dark corner of the room. Rick then went under the Ganzfeld after me and Jay stayed in the room with him.

Jay noted that Rick was very nervous. He felt as though something was walking around them, and Rick kept hearing voices that he couldn't identify. He didn't know if he was hearing talking among a large group of people or if several people were all trying to communicate with him.

So why did Jay and Beverly seem to get more out of their session? They're both more sensitive than myself, and I will admit that I am much more skeptical. So I wonder if it's like a self-fulfilling prophecy—if you don't believe in what you could be seeing, it won't happen. I tend to sometimes close myself off from paranormal experiences because I'm very much in the zone of trying to debunk my experiences along the way. I also find that when I let my guard down, disaster tends to happen as I lose control over the situation and turn into an irresponsible ghost hunter. There were many things happening on this night that could have caused me to lose my cool and let the night run wild. But I had to keep it together for the sake of my team.

While Rick and Jay were in the HQ room, Beverly and I sat in the stairwell and did an EVP session at the bottom of the flight on the second floor where Missy had reportedly died. The lights remained on because we didn't want to risk walking up and down the stairs in darkness. As we conducted our EVP session, we set out boundaries to not be physically touched.

What first caught our attention was the sound of rustling on the floor below us as if someone was in their office. I then decided to channel some good-old spiritualism techniques and asked the presence to make a noise by knocking on something. One tap for yes, two taps for no. And I asked questions about age and gender that made us believe that it was a young girl. I then asked, "Are you trapped here?"

There was no rapping, but the lights went out, and we were in pitch-black darkness in the stairwell.

I uttered some expletives and headed up the stairs to find that the automatic lighting had gone out. After a few laughs at ourselves for getting worked up, we sat back down and continued with our EVP session. Beverly then noted that she was getting a headache, and asked whatever we were communicating with if it was giving her a headache.

One tap. Yes.

It was then that I had to consider the safety of my team members. If whatever was here, whether it was Missy or someone else, was powerful enough to affect the physical human body, then what else was it capable of? The extent of how much a deceased human soul can do is still debated in the anomalous world, and there is a clear line between what a human ghost can do and something that we would consider to be inhuman. Religious circles would call this a demonic entity, while other circles would call it djinn, elemental, fae, and more.

Also while in the stairwell with Beverly, I noticed that it sounded busy downstairs, though it was a bit different than the last time. It sounded as if someone was tinkering in the offices below. There was movement with feet and the knocking continued as we asked questions with one and two knock-and-tap responses. For the purpose of consistency, I would ask the same questions twice in a row to make sure there wasn't some sort of pattern going on with the general sounds of the building. While I had never had a productive session like that before, I couldn't help but have doubts in my head while also being excited about the experiences we were having at the theater.

After reuniting with the guys, I decided that it was time to do an EVP session in that corner of the room where we felt like something was watching—the place where we were all legitimately creeped. Given that I had heard so much sound over there, it was something that I needed to investigate not only for my own sanity, but to quench the curiosity of my team.

A Reluctant Guest

I had never felt like I was invading someone's space before being in that corner. The overall oppressive feeling—like a weight on your chest and your head feeling like it was being squeezed—was almost overwhelming. And out of all the places around the theater, I was actually fearful—not just nervous. I can't explain why. Maybe it was an elevated level of EMF in that corner. I don't know.

Then I heard the rattling, like someone was walking on squeaky floorboards. But it was like someone was putting their foot on the same spot. We could feel the vibrations in the floor. So I decided to ask, "Can you do that again?"

Stomp.

"Can you do that two times in a row?"

Stomp stomp.

"Are you a man or a—"

Stomp.

"Are you kidding?"

At that moment, our one source of light in that corner was temporarily blocked out as a dark figure passed by the window.

"Well, that was interesting. It was almost like a figure was walking by." As I looked at the window, it happened again. I was actually frightened. Not only was the vibe of the room very tense, but I was seeing something with my naked eye that was dark.

"Oh my god . . . I can't look over there again," I declared.

"Can you share some emotions or personal information with me?" Beverly asked. I looked over at her and asked if she was sure she was ready to take on the challenge, and she nodded her head in agreement. Despite my better judgment, I allowed her to open herself up and continue.

"Are you angry that we're here?" Beverly asked.

Stomp.

"I'm getting the 'leave me alone, why do you need to know this information about me and don't worry about it' kind of feeling," said Beverly. As the temperature continued to drop, I couldn't get over the feeling that someone was looming over me. Watching, waiting, and with the anticipation to strike.

"Something just touched my head," I announced. While I welcome being touched during an EVP session, it doesn't make the feeling any less unsettling when it actually happens. It felt as though something was bopping me on the head telling me to shut up.

I asked the presence how old it was and whether or not it was Missy, the British Lieutenant, or the Baptist Pastor.

None. No answer at all. It contradicted all of the previous noise that had occurred. This told me that we were dealing with a ghost that was very much aware of its surroundings and who they were talking to. We possibly have a fourth unidentified person haunting the Tenth, and he was not in a good mood and didn't like that we were there asking him questions.

I tried to change the mood by asking general questions about how it felt about the building being used as a theater, and what it thought about the partying going on outside on an ongoing basis. It was then that the mood changed.

"I'm still feeling agitated, but the feeling is reducing and going away slowly," said Beverly. And the stomping and squeaking sounds stopped. I beckoned Beverly to take a moment to see if whatever presence was there was willing to communicate with her silently. As she listened, she nodded her head and made audial cues that she was understanding what was being told to her. While there were no more responses to my questions, it was comfortable with Beverly. She then informed me and the team that the presence was a male in his fifties. At that moment, I felt as though the angry presence that was once with us had left. Perhaps we were speaking to the Baptist Pastor, and the emotions we were feeling was the resentment he felt toward himself and the overwhelming guilt he felt over the death of Missy.

I ended the EVP session and took the team all the way down to the basement where Jeff said there was reported activity. He also mentioned that the same psychic who picked up on the British Lieutenant in the main stage was drawn to the basement, stating that the spirit of a young boy was occupying in that space. Jeff was hoping to turn the basement into a wine cellar and be a place where people could do wine tastings. The basement was still under construction, and we had to use a ladder to get down into the space.

The basement was a small, cramped, L-shaped space. The long part of the room had a large wooden sliding door on the left side, and there was a puddle of water on the floor. I didn't feel anything weird in this space. The rest of my team members had no weird feelings or anything. But we proceeded with an EVP session, which yielded no response that we could hear with our ears. Even going back and listening to the audio, I heard and got nothing.

However, just because there is no response and you get nothing, doesn't mean that the space isn't occupied. I would quickly learn that on my third visit to the Tenth.

A Girl Confused

After a long night, I decided that it was time to call it a night. We headed back up to our HQ room to pack up our tech and to put the room back to the way it was when we found it, and then headed down to the lobby. I realized that we hadn't done our closing duties of checking the light switches to make sure that they were completely off.

"Ah man, we have to go return the key to the fourth floor," Jay remembered.

He and Rick tried the old antique elevator to see if it would work, but to no avail. So they reluctantly went up the stairs to the fourth floor while Beverly and I waited in the lobby. Both of us were tired and just talking about how productive the investigation was. I then made a joke about how it would be funny if the guys came back down running and screaming like in *Scooby-Doo*. Well, be careful what you say.

We heard the guys yelling and jumping down flights of stairs. Breathless, we saw Jay and Rick running down the last flight of stairs and hunched over as they were catching their breath and Rick saying, "No no no no no no" with each step he took.

"We totally just heard a little girl's voice saying, 'Mommy!'" gasped Jay.

"No way … what floor were you on?" I asked.

"The sound was behind us. We were on the fourth floor, and it sounded like it was right there behind us saying 'Mommy,'" Jay said.

It was then I realized that it was on the fourth floor where Beverly and I kept seeing that shadow wandering up and down the hall and peeking into the room. I had chills up spine, especially since Beverly had a theory that it was Missy looking for her mother. And then Jay and Rick go up to the fourth floor by themselves and hear the word, "Mommy" in a child's voice. I'm not one to believe in coincidences. And considering that the guys had their guard down when they were returning the key, plus being it was the end of the night, they were caught at the perfect time. I felt bad that they ran back down and that they didn't engage with the voice at the moment. But they were new to the field; technically this was Rick's very first investigation. He certainly dove in headfirst and got much more than he ever bargained for.

"That poor girl was confused," Beverly commented.

"It sounded like a girl looking for her mommy though," Rick said.

"I hate to ask this, but did you guys check the light switches as you were running down?" I asked.

I ended up not sending them back up there. Quickly, I decided to head upstairs to check the lights. I kept an extra ear out for anything strange. As each floor was illuminated once again, the stress and the tension seemed to disappear away with the darkness. I stayed on each flight of stairs for a few minutes to make sure the lights shut off when they were supposed to. As I waited, I was tickled at the fact that the ghost of a kid could send two military men running. I hoped that I would have been treated with the same experience, but I was greeted with silence. For a first time visit to the Tenth, I got more than just a few glances of possible phenomenon, I had an actual conversation with those from the other side, and I couldn't wait to go back.

Six

THE RETURN

In the seven months between the first and the second investigation at the Tenth, the team had a rush of cases come in. Considering that we were still a fairly new team (about a year old at this point), I was glad the team was getting some fieldwork in. Leading a team of new people is a very trying task until your members get up to speed. I try to train my team to be self-sufficient, meaning that they don't need to depend on me to get a case done. As the new cases began to come in, I noticed that weird things in my house would start to occur, such as strange noises, shadows out of the corner of my eye, and phantom voices. I noticed that right before a new case would come in, the odd occurrences would begin, but they would end a few days later.

Taking Work Home

Of course, paranormal experiences in the house I was living in wasn't all that new to me, as I had a few experiences in the room I was sleeping in at the time. But I began to have experiences at home that reminded me of the first investigation at the Tenth. I don't know how to explain this besides saying that the same feeling and vibe that I got on the fourth floor at the Tenth was present in my bedroom and living room, the two places I frequented most often when at home. As I woke up in the middle of the night to take care of my kittens, sometimes my eyes would play tricks on me and I would see a young girl in the corner of my room with dark hair and curious eyes wanting to know what I was doing. On some nights, I would see a more sinister shadow looming over my bed in front of my window, causing me to see nothing but a black silhouette. When that happened, I was unable to speak or move—only stunned to see what was around me. The same feeling of anger, dread, and tension was present. Had something that followed me home seven months ago stayed dormant until now?

I never spoke to my team about these experiences. I wasn't purposely trying to keep a secret, but I felt that those experiences were only meant for me, and not to be repeated to others. I found that whenever I thought about the Tenth or was speaking to Jeff about returning for an investigation or a theater project, the experiences would return. I don't believe that the ghosts of the Tenth are trapped or bound to the building. I believe they have the ability to travel, and I was ready to entertain the idea that perhaps they were visiting me in my home before I went to go see them in their home in order to level the playing field.

I was finally able to work an investigation at the Tenth into my schedule, as well as my team members' schedules. It seemed like there was never the right time to get the team over there. With the Tenth becoming a booming place and getting booked on a regular basis, we also had to work around the schedules of renters and tenants. This time around, Jeff contacted me the week before the investigation to tell me that someone from the local news station was going to be at the Tenth to do some promotional work for the annual "Terror at the Tenth" film festival, which takes place every fall. I was completely okay with it since we had the building for the night and even if we were delayed, we could make up for the lost time later into the night.

The Second Date

I contacted the team to let them know what equipment to bring, and I also arranged to interview a man named Gus, a new potential team member at the Tenth. Based on my previous conversations with Gus and his application, I was fairly sure that I was going to take him on, and figured he could do a test investigation at the theater. What better way to see if a potential member would be a good match than to have him investigate with us at an active location? I was very excited about this possibility. When I gave Gus the address, I had asked him if he was familiar with the building, and he wasn't. Fresh eyes were about to set upon the Tenth.

Upon arrival, I saw Gus waiting in front of the Tenth, dressed in a suit and tie. I felt bad about my casual outfit, which was a black skirt and a purple top, as well as having the hair of a drowned rat. I knocked on the door and Jeff let us in. We took a seat in the lobby/ground-level area, and we were met with numerous people who were still in the Tenth even though it was after ten o'clock. As I pulled out my notebook so I could take notes during Gus's interview, Jeff approached me and asked me if I was willing to be interviewed on camera about the ghosts at the Tenth and show off some of the equipment that we use. Apparently word about the Tenth being haunted was beginning to spread, and I was the only investigator who had looked into the building. Wide-eyed, I agreed, but then I remembered that I looked like a mess, and that I wasn't "camera ready." The reporter agreed to give me ten minutes to freshen up and wait for my other team members, who had the tech equipment, to arrive. While waiting for Jay and Beverly, I stepped back inside the theater to continue my interview with Gus. He was brand new to the paranormal field and wanted to learn more about the unknown along with helping people. I made him aware that we end up debunking more hauntings than we solve, and Gus was okay with that. I found him to be young and extraordinarily down-to-earth. He was enthusiastic and had a thirst for knowledge. I had a good feeling about him and invited him to stick around for the investigation. I heard a knock at the door, and there was Jay standing in the doorway. He looked concerned and I asked him what was wrong.

"So ... Bev locked the tech in the car," Jay said.

"Um ... okay? So get it out," I replied.

"The ... keys ... are also locked in the car," he said.

"What?"

So the team's tech equipment was locked in a car, and I had to start the on-camera interview in just a few minutes. Jay made a point to mention that this had never happened before and it was an extraordinary situation. I asked him if he felt that perhaps this was paranormal-related, and he looked at me with confirmation. I told him to do what he needed to get the tech out of the car while I did the interview.

By the time the interview was over, Jay and Beverly were able to get into their car and get all of the tech equipment out. (They ended up calling a locksmith.) As we started our setup process, I invited Gus to stay and learn how to set up the cameras and do preliminary checks around the building to get baseline readings. Sometimes our setup itself can take about one to two hours, as baseline readings of only a few seconds aren't acceptable, and it takes a considerable amount of time sitting and monitoring fluctuations with the electricity alone. Gus was eager, even though he was dressed formally.

After the camera crew packed up and left, Jeff wished us a good investigation and went home. With glee, I galloped to the writing room and set our equipment up. Jay was showing Gus the ropes of setting up the cameras, and just the very fact that we amped up our technical inventory made me very excited for the night's investigation. No more would we miss unexplainable moments because of a lack of equipment. Instead, we would be able to capture every moment. With better equipment, I knew that our ongoing research into the Tenth would continue with more credibility.

Perhaps my pride was already a warning that the evening would not go the way I planned.

A Rocky Start

First of all, there were people still hanging about in the building. Of course, the Tenth was host to several businesses and organizations that rented their offices, so they had a right to be in there as much as they wanted. It didn't make me any less annoyed as I heard footsteps coming down the stairs and noises being made, which I took note of and nearly lost all hope that we would be able to capture any substantial audio evidence. As the midnight hour was approaching, I kept walking by the occupied office and wondering why the heck someone would be in there that late unless they were on deadline or working on a massive project.

Finally, the occupant of the office went down the stairs and departed, but not before seeing my team with the tech equipment and giving us some funny looks. The worker was also probably wondering why we were in the building so late at night, though I recognized the face as someone who was around the first time we investigated the Tenth as well as the times I was in the theater to work on my staged reading.

As we set up shop in the writing room, I held back my information and experiences from Gus, mainly because I didn't want to taint his own time in the theater alone. I didn't want to "prime" him, so to speak, by letting him know what to expect in each room, which could make him overly paranoid or observant and have paranormal experiences that may not have been real.

After setup was completed, we were finally ready to begin the investigation. As we opened up the floor in the same way as we did before, there was an odd feeling about the building. But it was a different feeling than I had before. There was no other living person in the building, but it also felt like the dead had taken a break from their appearance tonight.

The only sounds we heard were coming from the outside as late-night weekday partiers were making their way to their cars and trying to get taxicabs for their ride home. I could hear conversations outside; I could even hear the wind inside of the writing room. But we didn't hear the footsteps that we had heard before. We continued to ask questions and tried to re-create our last investigation along with re-creating a "typical evening" at the theater acting as techs or actors working on lines. We got nothing. I found it weird, but then Beverly spoke up.

"They're not wanting to come out tonight. They're hearing, but they're not in the mood to converse," she announced. At that moment, I realized that she wasn't as talkative as our first trip to the Tenth.

I shrugged it off, thinking that maybe her intuition was off or maybe she was just tired and wanted to leave early. This evening did have a weird start with the interview and the television crew and then having the tech locked in the car for an hour, delaying our setup, plus the lone office worker who took a long time to leave the building. Maybe as a whole, the team wasn't really ready for tonight, and seeing this, the ghosts weren't interested in interacting with us.

A Different Approach

So, after thirty minutes of not getting much interaction, I decide to take the group to the roof, where we had the experience of the door opening by itself. The roof wasn't nearly as windy as it was on our first visit. It was breezy, but we didn't need our jackets. At this point, Jay decided that he wanted to bring out his laser-grid pen and turn it onto the stairwell that led to the roof doorway. If something had opened the door before, then surely there could be the potential for another appearance since the mysterious figure would probably pass through that stairwell to get to the door. As Jay turned on the laser grid, we set up the camera to face the stairwell and the hundreds of green dots in the dark. I won't lie; just looking at that by itself was a little creepy. So, with the camera and laser grid set up a few steps below us, the five of us sat close together and began talking to whatever presence was there.

If you have never used a laser grid before in a paranormal investigation, essentially it is a movement tracker. If you walk through a laser grid, the dots will move to your body. Think of a time that you moved in front of an overhead projector either in school, at work, or in a movie theater. So basically, if an apparition walks in front of that laser grid and made the dots move, it would indicate that it had mass. There has been much debate in the paranormal world as to whether ghosts have mass. Considering the big boom when it comes to orb and apparition photos (90 percent of them are debunkable as dust, moisture, etc.), if we're able to see an apparition with our naked eye, is there some sort of mass reflecting the light to create its shape or is it something that is being projected out of our subconscious? Well, the laser grid is a good place to start in trying to find out that answer.

As we sat, we asked questions and attempted to re-create the events on the roof, yet we were still experiencing no activity. It was very disheartening, and I was beginning to think that Gus was probably thinking that this team was a bust. I then decided it was time to try out a new area of the Tenth: the gallery.

When we got up to pack up and head downstairs, we started to hear voices down the stairwell.

"What was that?" I asked.

Jay quickly shushed me as he held his hand up, like a conductor getting ready to lead his orchestra into the next phase of music. Gus, Beverly, Rick, and I stood with silent anticipation as the muffled voices made their presence known once more.

"We're the only ones in the building, right?" Beverly looked concerned.

"Yes. We're supposed to be alone. The door is locked so no one can get in unless they have a key," I replied.

These voices didn't sound like they came from an adult, but instead, they sounded like a group of children playing a game. The sounds sent chills up my spine. There was also the possibility that the voices were those of high-pitched women. Needing to know the answer sooner rather than later, I grabbed what I could and I raced down the dark stairs with the team scrambling after me.

As I raced down the flights of stairs with only my flashlight in tow, my eyes were adjusting and I could see my reflection in the paintings that were hung on the walls of the landings. In my rushed fury, I looked straight into the glass of each painting onto my reflection. A few times, I thought I saw more faces than just my own. There were moments that I thought I saw a dark-haired girl, who was shorter than me, just looming behind me. I wanted to confirm the sighting, but I was in a rush, and in my short seconds of panic, I didn't want to stop. The voices continued to travel down the stairs, and I felt like I was on a wild goose chase and the voice was laughing at me for the fact that I fell for their game.

What were we experiencing? Was it a conscious spirit taking us on this game, or was it an imprint of energy from the past? Missy's death happened in a similar scenario where she played a chasing game down the stairs before meeting her death. I wondered if this was a moment that had such emotional significance that it ended up being embedded in the walls of the Tenth.

There was a concept presented in the 1970s called the Stone Tape Theory, which embodied the idea that inanimate objects could absorb the energy during moments of emotional significance, such as a fight or the end of someone's life. Eleanor Mildred Sidgwick, who was one of the earliest psychical researchers, did her work in the late 1800s to early 1900s and was even named President of the Society for Psychical Research in 1908, first proposed the concept. Other researchers such as William G. Roll would show their support for the theory as well, stating that all humans are carriers of something called "psi fields," which are responsible for carrying psi information to our minds. To sum up this paragraph simply, the human mind is powerful enough to leave psychic traces during intense moments. There is no doubt that the occurrence of Missy's death was traumatizing, and it is a wonder to consider that perhaps the shock and grief of the Pastor, those in the building, and Missy's friends and family, were powerful enough to leave an emotional imprint. Ghost hunters and paranormal investigators have also called this phenomenon a "residual haunting." This type of phenomenon is unconscious, which means that I could definitely notice its presence, but it would not interact with me like an intelligent haunting would.

As I was chasing the voice down the stairs, I wondered if I was chasing a residual haunting. At this moment I realized that I had spent so much time focusing on the "intelligent" spirits that I nearly forgot the possibility that we could be dealing with a residual haunting.

Subtle Signs

As I stopped at the bottom of the stairs on the third floor, I saw something that greatly confused me. Along with the writing room and the gallery, there was also a gym. If you were going up the stairs from the lobby, the gym would be straight in front of you, and then you would need to turn left to reach the writing room and the gallery (which was at the end of the hall). Whenever we have been in the building, the gym room was closed, as it is owned by another business and they are usually gone by the time we arrive. This includes visits for investigations, performances, and rehearsals. Inside, the lights are motion activated.

When we all arrived at the Tenth on this night, regardless of interviews taking place or setup, I made sure to take note of the gym room since two lights tend to stay on continuously, with a motion sensor light in between them. As a standard practice in our investigations, I usually make note of the light situation as I turn off the lights in the Tenth as an attempt to reduce some of the electrical energy swirling around the building. So as I reached the third floor, what did I see?

The motion sensor light in the gym was on.

This was the first time I had ever seen all of the lights on inside of the gym. Given that this was our second investigation and my total visits inside of the Tenth had reached double-digits, this was a significant moment for me. I wasn't sure exactly what the timer was like, but considering the layout and management of the building, it was likely on the same timer as the stair lights. Like with the laser grid, if something set off the motion-sensor light, whatever was in there must have had some sort of mass to trigger the switch. It could have been a rat, a bug (depending how sensitive the light was), maybe all of our footsteps from rushing down the stairs set the light on, or it very well could have been something else that we couldn't explain.

Because we didn't have access to the gym, there wasn't much we could do to try to debunk the light situation at the time. It would have to be something that I would follow up on with Jeff at a later date. That particular space was not ours to explore. So I then moved the crew into the art gallery, which was a large room with wooden floors. As we walked down the hall toward the room, I looked back just in time to see the motion light in the gym turn off.

The art gallery was empty with no new displays and nothing on the walls. So it was a completely blank room. I grabbed my laptop and red lights and decided it was time to at least try the Ganzfeld experiment in the gallery—we had a completely empty room at our disposal, why not try some experimentation with parapsychology?

The art gallery at the theater. Courtesy of Jeff Cotta.

Since the Ganzfeld experiment altered our state of consciousness and emulated a dream-like state, I was distinctly hoping that this would open our minds up to communication from an intelligent spirit or even just a vision of an event from the past. At this point, I would have been satisfied with classic rapping from the Spiritualism method.

In his fashion of wanting to always be the brave one, Jay went first. This time around, the rest of us stayed in the room with him, since it was big enough to observe the experiment from a distance. It was also beneficial because I could then explain the experiment to Gus. Before we began, Jay also set up his rem-pod, which is a little round device with an antennae and several little lights. It is an EMF detector that will go off with lights and sounds if something with an electric current gets near the antennae. So if you were to put your hand near the device, it will go off. While I know the relationship between ghosts and EMF is controversial and has yet to be proven, I would love to see the rem-pod go off by itself at some point of my paranormal career. Even if it were debunked by natural causes, it would still be neat to see the actions of EMF at work before my eyes.

As Jay was asking questions to the unseen ghosts at the Tenth, we continued to wait on the side. As we observed him, the gallery felt like an empty void of space. I had never felt a sensation such as that before. My disappointment in the evening was growing stronger.

After Jay was done, he experienced the usual activity associated with the Ganzfeld in terms of what the body naturally experiences after having parts of your senses taken away, such as voices through the white noise, someone walking around him, and light sensations that emulate being touched. Now, I have been touched during the Ganzfeld session, but after numerous sessions, one has to learn the differences in sensations. There is the light tingling sensation as your nerves adjust to the new state of mind, as well as feeling a bit colder, which I feel comes when you stop moving and sit still. Your body's temperature will go down naturally. This is why when people report feeling cold fairly shortly after starting a communication session, I take it with a grain of salt. Reinforcing the temperature change with a thermometer or temperature gun is a good idea for these types of situations.

While I was disappointed in Jay's session, I asked Gus if he wanted to give it a go, and he agreed enthusiastically. As I got him set up and ready to go, we decided to officially let him on the team. It was pretty much a unanimous decision, as Gus was not only enthusiastic but also open-minded and understanding when it seemed like there was no activity occurring in the building. Paranormal investigators spend a lot of their time debunking hauntings, and sometimes you have to tell your client that they need an electrician in their house instead of a ghost hunting team. I would rather have someone on the team with that sort of mind-set instead of someone who will try to make any experience seem paranormal. Also, when taking on a new member, you have to be able to trust them 110 percent. If you're going to be approaching an intense haunting that has the potential to turn negative, you want to make sure that your team members have your back.

I told Gus to talk during his session and report on whether he was experiencing anything strange. I also explained to him that we were using the Ganzfeld to communicate with spirits, not test out any kind of telepathy or communication with the mind. The fact that this was being used as an attempt toward spirit communication was a shot in the dark. For Gus's first time, he did really well. It was an uneventful session in terms of trying to establish communication, but Gus was also trying to get his bearings and get acquainted with the equipment. Could there have been something he missed? Certainly. Beverly and Rick went under the Ganzfeld as well, and it was uneventful. What was interesting was that neither of them experienced even stereotypical Ganzfeld occurrences like the shadows, the touching, or the faint voices. It was almost like someone hit a switch to turn "everything" off, so to speak.

A Second Chance

As we walked down the stairs, Jay suggested that we try the basement before taking off. I figured since we had the building for a little while longer, might as well make the trip down. Even though our first trip didn't produce many results when it came to responses in a paranormal aspect, I had to remain optimistic that something could still happen.

My current mind-set left me neutral because I really didn't know if the night would end with any kind of communication between the team and the ghosts at the Tenth. So far the evidence that we had collected were faces in the glass, voices (that could have been coming from the outside), and a motion light that mysteriously turned on all by itself. When it came to having significant experiences, the first trip was definitely the more active investigation. But also, with this literally "dead" night, I worried that this evening would also counter any progress that was made from the first investigation. Was the first trip just a fluke? That question continued to plague my mind like a monkey on my back that was questioning me non-stop. But it was also common for investigations to have quiet nights.

As I guided Gus down the steep set of stairs, I told him about our experiences from the first trip to the Tenth, and while he was disappointed that this current trip wasn't all that exciting and active, he suggested that perhaps maybe this could be evidence that there really were ghosts at the Tenth. I looked at him with initial confusion.

"Well, think about it," he said. "If the occurrences that you guys experienced were consistent with the changes in the environment, that would debunk the footsteps, and essentially your entire first trip would have been a waste. But since tonight is silent, maybe it means that whatever was causing the craziness from the first night decided to take a break tonight."

That sliver of input cemented Gus's spot on the team.

First, I was impressed with Gus's observations and wisdom. Second, he had a point. Maybe the ghosts of the Tenth decided to take the night off, or they didn't expect a second trip and therefore wanted to stay quiet. Or maybe they just didn't want to be bothered. Who knows? Or, perhaps they were unimpressed with me getting interviewed by the media several hours before the investigation.

So the rest of the team made their way down to the basement, and we all stood or sat wherever there was room. If there are more than three people in the basement, it gets pretty cozy, and we had about five people with us. Immediately upon getting down there, we felt colder. It was a mild fall evening, and the rest of the building was temperature regulated, so I imagined that it would be a little colder in the basement. But this was near freezing temperature, and those of us who didn't have a jacket started shivering. We could actually see our breath. For this California-raised girl, that was pretty damn cold.

I decided that now was a time to conduct an EVP session—before the moment was lost. Based on my previous experiences in the field, if the temperature was dropping that significantly, then it was quite possibly someone wanting to communicate with us. You could cut the tension in the basement with a knife, and I remembered Jeff telling me about the psychic who picked up on a ghost in the basement. I wondered if the silent spirit from the first trip had finally decided it was time to make an appearance. Things began to move around and sounds were heard while the team was standing as still as a pile of boards. As we conducted the EVP session in our usual fashion of seeking responses through taps and knocks, Beverly got a feeling that we were in the presence of a playful child. If you have ever been in a dark room with a hidden person, where they were making noises and forcing you to guess where they were, then you have an idea of what we were experiencing in the basement.

From the responses we got by asking questions and requesting answers in the form of sounds, it seemed as though we were speaking to the spirit of a young boy. At that moment, I wished that we had brought a toy for him to play with because as soon as he started talking to us, I realized we had the potential to make a deeper connection. We were then met with silence, so we waited a few more minutes, giving the spirit one more chance to make his presence more prominent, before finally leaving the basement. And I was relieved that we experienced something there and established communication with a different presence.

We conducted our closing circle in case someone or something was inspired to follow us home. As we returned the key as Jeff instructed us, I shut the door behind us, looked up at the windows, and wondered how this investigation was different from our first investigation. Why didn't Missy come out this time around? Why didn't the presence of the Fourth-Floor Theater (also called the Forum Theater) make it clear this time around that he didn't want us in there? Did I do something to make the ghosts not want to ever come out again? Well, I suppose that it wouldn't be a terrible thing and perhaps they could move on and find peace.

Worn Out

This got me to thinking: if the haunting at the Tenth became a huge deal and people started to investigate the building on a regular basis, what would it mean for the ghosts in this building? If they didn't like the extra attention, would they move on into the light or leave the building? I honestly wasn't sure, and the fact that we had a dead night in a very haunted location made me question my own motives for wanting to keep coming back to the Tenth. Maybe the ghosts just want to be left alone and be more in control of their interactions with the living. Maybe they like to be the ones approaching the world instead of the other way around. Maybe investigating the Tenth was a disrespectful action against the dead and perhaps this was my sign to just leave it be.

All I could say at this point was that a third trip to the Tenth would be in order. It honestly felt like this story was not over yet.

The Return ... Once Again

It would be a while before I was able to return to the Tenth for another investigation. However, I did go to the building several more times as an actor and an audience member. Perhaps I was feeling some betrayal from this second trip to the point where I didn't even want to hear the words "ghost" and "the Tenth" in the same sentence. Even with the shadows in the corner of my eye and hearing the voices down the hallways, I wanted a break from the ghosts. I was done feeling foolish over experiencing paranormal phenomenon only to have it be debunked. And also around that time, my team was experiencing a surge in cases and our personal lives were taking us away from investigating.

I had to start doing a lot of soul searching within myself. Perhaps I was also being dramatic and overreacting to the fact that I didn't have the amazing experience that I had the first time in the building, and I was reacting like a spoiled brat. I needed to do some growing up before returning to the Tenth. I had never felt like I failed before or that I really made any huge mistakes while investigating and confirming whether a location was haunted. While I had experiences that evening, and there were spooky things occurring, at the end of the night, we hadn't captured any substantial evidence nor had any experiences that we could confidently confirm.

What would our next step be in my journey with the Tenth Avenue Arts Center? For one, a return trip was necessary. I had to decide whether trip one or trip two was the fluke. Second, I had to reassess the way that I approached the investigation. And third, I had to change my attitude about the Tenth and learn to be more cautious before jumping on the bandwagon that a location was haunted or not. This was a learning experience in becoming a more thorough researcher and the need to step up my process of spirit communication. I was at a fork in the road of my paranormal career. I could take the disappointing night and consider it a sign to hang up the investigator hat, or I could start working harder.

Lord knows that after that night, life quickly got in the way again with work, client cases, and my extracurricular work in theater. But with each case that came up, I would still see those mysterious figures in my room in the middle of the night, with that familiar feeling in the room … reminding me that the ghosts of the Tenth were still there and waiting for the time when I would come back and start paying attention to them again.

Seven

SECOND CHANCES

Five more months went by after that second trip. The interview from that night aired on television and now lives immortally on YouTube and the news outlet's website. Overall, it got good feedback with the occasional naysayer saying that ghosts weren't real. Soon enough, the Tenth began to creep back into my life. Since I was getting ready to move to North Carolina in a few months for a new job, I wanted to investigate there one more time before leaving the West Coast. Interestingly enough, the team got a generous donation from our community members so we could book a space for our Meetup about poltergeists. One of the goals of the team was to create a network of members around the San Diego area that discussed the paranormal and investigated together. Because of this addition, my immediate team members which included Jay, Beverly, Gus, and now David (our newest member and resident psychic), I renamed them the "core members" since they took on the client cases with me. Rick unfortunately had a to take a step back from the team because the paranormal was hitting too close to home for him, and he wanted to protect his wife and children from anything that could be brought home. Nothing had happened yet, but he really didn't want to find out.

The community members supported our team, attended our monthly talks religiously, and provided moral and financial support, which helped us reach more clients around Southern California. The community members were just that—members of the paranormal community around town. They supported different teams, and it was an honor to be included in their list of "go to" teams to check out. As a thank you to those community members, I thought…why not get them into the Tenth? None of them had ever investigated the Tenth, but many had wanted to and would have if they had the connections to make it happen. I decided to be that connection.

A Larger Setting

I contacted Jeff to pitch the idea, and he loved it. I wasn't going to charge the community members for the time at the theater, and so, we were all set to go the next weekend. I sent private messages and e-mails to each community member with an invitation, and we were going to have about ten people at the theater. Of course, I was a little nervous because this was the first time that my team was going to host an investigation for the public, but also I was worried that the same thing would happen as the last trip—that there would be little action.

This time around, I was also going to have several psychics in the building at once. In total, three people would have some kind of mediumship abilities. I wanted to give each of them enough time in the building before the rest of the group arrived, as I wanted to hear what each of them had to say about the space and who was haunting it.

As I parked my car, Jay and Beverly pulled up in the spot beside me, and we gathered our bags and suitcases of tech equipment. I knocked on the door and Jeff once again greeted me with a smile. I also saw that some of the community members had arrived early, and I gently reminded them that they wouldn't be able to come in yet. I decided that the three psychic mediums would have free rein of the building for about thirty minutes so they could do a walk-through. Jay and I would shadow them and take notes of their observations. I also kept in mind that the stories of the Tenth ghosts were on the Internet, so in a small way, they were already tainted. But I was open to hearing what they had to say, and I was more interested in whether the psychics could pick up the personal experiences of the team and others who had disclosed their encounters to Jeff or myself.

A Psychic View

This would be the first time the Tenth had a psychic in the building since Jeff brought his in all those years ago. I was

fortunate enough to have met David at one of our community meetings, and he expressed a strong interest in being a
part of the team. After an interview, a background check, and
a test read, I felt his goals aligned with the team's mission of
helping others.

But David was not the first psychic to work with the team.
Rommel Lozano was the first psychic to work consistently with
the team as an on-call guest. This meant that he wasn't an official core member, but his skills and abilities were highly sought
after, and he made himself available to assist with our cases
as we needed him. Rommel was so strict in his policy of not
being tainted that I would actually drive him to the case with
absolutely no information. Without any hints, he would pick
up on traits of the client cases, and he also assisted with resolu-
tions. Along with being a reliable connection in the paranormal community, he had also become one of my good friends.

The last medium we called in was Madison. While I
had never worked with her before, she came highly recommended by David and Rommel. And if they believed in her
abilities and trusted her, then I needed to give her a shot.

As Rommel, Madison, and David came in, I could tell that
they were anxious to get started. I explained to the three mediums that they would go around the building by themselves, but
that Madison would be escorted by Jay, I would escort Rommel, and David would roam by himself, since he was an official
team member and would adhere to our policies and protocol
by contract. I wanted all three psychics to work by themselves

because I didn't want them to share or exchange information, which would influence their entire experience. And the reason I commonly use more than one psychic is because I've found that no one works exactly the same way. Some persons with abilities can predict the future or be like Beverly and feel emotions. Or they could work remotely and see images far away from a distance. With such an array of psychic abilities, I felt that integrating as many people with abilities as possible would help in the gathering of information on the Tenth.

I observed Rommel as he twiddled his fingers in excitement, as if the ghosts were already speaking to him. Madison got out her dowsing rods and began to walk around the building. David closed his eyes and took a deep breath as he started to work on his own. I noticed that all three of the psychics were attracted to the lighting booth, where I had the unexplainable experience of the lights going down at my staged reading. I found that to be interesting.

For the purpose of keeping the traffic around the lighting booth clear, I momentarily stuck around as Rommel waited on the landing of the stairs below us.

"There is someone in there who watches and observes what goes on around here," Madison said as she observed the lighting booth, gently running her fingers over the railing. I glanced at Jay, and his eyes looked to me like he wasn't surprised that Madison would have picked up on whoever was there.

I tried to remain neutral as the psychics were walking around, as I didn't want to tip them off and give them any false impressions. As I walked with Rommel, he picked up on the presence of a young girl, and said that she liked to mess with people who were in the hallways. He kept going to the flight of stairs that led up to the fourth floor and noted it as the place where the young girl was most active.

David reported to me that he picked up on the same presence in the lighting booth as Madison, as well as the presence of a young girl.

The Group Assembles

Eventually, it was time to let the rest of the group in, and I told Jay to have them gather on the main stage. With almost a dozen faces looking at me with excited eyes, I told the group that I was planning being very regimented during the night's investigation and gave them some basic rules for being in the space. I asked everyone if they had any questions, which they did not. I also let the group know that they would be broken up into smaller groups with Jay and I as leaders. Our goal was to take each group into the places where we had experienced activity and keep at least a floor in between each group to avoid tainting the evidence and paranormal experiences.

We decided to have everyone start in the main stage area. I was pleased to see how cooperative everyone was and that they each had a buddy with them as they got out their technical equipment. Then I gave them the lowdown of the building as well as my expectations.

The main stage of the Tenth Avenue. Courtesy of Jeff Cotta.

"I run a tight ship here. Because there are businesses here as well as theater-related projects taking place on a regular basis, essentially you can't walk around the building by yourself and you need an APS member with you at all times," I announced.

As I looked at the group's eager faces, I wanted to make once more announcement:

"We have had a mix of experiences here as well as nothing happening at all. This night can go in many different directions and while I don't want to discount what I have experienced here, I don't want to get your hopes up either." I didn't want them to expect anything in terms of having a paranormal experience. Heck, I learned during the last trip that there is a strong possibility that nothing will happen at all and the night would be a bust.

Before I put people into their groups, I wanted to get a feel for personalities and who got along with each other, which is why we would all start by investigating the main stage, the area known as the sanctuary from when the building was a chapel and where there were reports of the presence of the British Lieutenant. I figured, why not? As a reportedly haunted hotspot in the Tenth, it was a good place to start because I could walk around and observe behaviors and investigation techniques.

I noticed that much of the group was gathering around a spot on the right side of the stage (from the audience's view of the stage). David said that there was a military admiral or lieutenant standing over there sending him images of his life and work. I also had a few of the non-psychic attendees tell me that they saw a black figure watching them from the lighting booth. Then I saw about three or four small groups dispersed around the main stage and the backstage area conducting their own EVP sessions. After about twenty minutes, I announced that we would now break into our groups and climb up the stairs to our destinations. I knew there were a few people who would need to use the old antique elevator, and I was a bit nervous about that, but that ended up turning out just fine.

First Contact

Jay agreed to have his group start on the roof while my group started in the writing room, where we had heard the mysterious footsteps almost a year before. Upon entering the writing room, I noticed that the table and chairs were gone. The cabinets and mirrors on the side were still there, but now there was a good deal of open floor and an armchair to the side. One of the community members, Ann, brought her hunting camera and set it up in the corner. Everyone got out their audio devices and placed them in the middle of our circle. As everyone was sitting, we had Rommel and David with us. I was a bit nervous at the idea of having two psychics in the same group, but I figured I would go along with it and reel them in as needed.

As we sat in the circle and began our EVP session, the temperature dropped quickly—to the point that we could see our breath. This was a new experience for me in that room. During the first investigation, it was certainly cold at our headquarters, but we couldn't see our breath. It was the middle of March in San Diego. It is usually in the mid-sixties, upper-seventies during this time of year, with little moisture in the air. All of the windows were shut, and the air conditioning had been on for most of the evening, but the room actually felt like it dropped down to the thirties. I actually began to feel excited again because it seemed that the ghosts were now going to come out and play.

"I'm seeing a man with a moustache, dressed in clothing from the 1800s," Rommel said.

"I'm actually getting the image of a woman in a Victorian-style dress," David chimed in.

I thought it interesting that two psychics, who I knew well and respected, were getting different people. Now, from an outsider perspective, the conflicting conclusions could be interpreted as both of them being wrong, but I saw this as another opportunity to dig deeper. Psychics generally have different variations of gifts, from being able to speak to dead people, reading people's emotions, seeing images of the past, or being able to speak of events in the future. Could it be that David and Rommel were executing their different gifts and picking up on people who were in different planes of existence? I didn't want to shut these two down, so I decided to push this further.

"Can you ask them to show you who else is in this building?" I asked.

Once this occurred, we began to hear knocking around the room, as if someone was walking along the walls and knocking in response.

"They would rather just talk to you," Rommel said.

That shocked me. I looked at David, who nodded in response. So I decided to start asking questions.

"Okay, we're going to play a game ... if I ask you a question, knock once for yes and—"

A knock interrupted me.

"So you understand what I'm asking you?"

One knock.

"Can you knock two times for no?"

Two knocks.

But this time they sounded like they were happening right behind me. These knocks weren't just regular knocks or sounds in an old building. They really did sound like someone was standing right in your space and knocking on the wall with their knuckles. Almost like they were saying, "Okay, I'm listening. No more games."

"Are you a man?"

One knock.

"Are you trapped here in this building?"

Two knocks.

"Is this your room?"

One knock.

Rommel then chimed in: "This is definitely his room, and he gets irritated by a young girl that comes in here. She's not allowed in this room."

Missy?

"Do you know about Missy?"

One knock.

"Why isn't she allowed in this room?"

Rommel then interrupted.

"She is too playful. She mainly hangs out in the staircase. She is always playing a game," he said. So perhaps it's possible that Missy still had rules and limitations in the afterlife, and that she wasn't allowed to roam as freely as I thought she could.

This also caused me to start thinking about where ghosts gravitate after they pass away. Missy seems to be really attracted to the area where she died, along with roaming the halls of the Tenth. Without knowing the story of her personal life or details of her family dynamics, we can only go by assumptions and theories. Perhaps the church was a positive place for her, where she had very positive memories despite being the location where she died. When we are introduced to a large space, or even a large group of people, we tend to gravitate toward what is the most comfortable for us.

I noticed that the Victorian woman David mentioned was being rather silent, so I was beginning to think that maybe she was more of a residual ghost, meaning that she wasn't a conscious soul, but instead an energy imprint of an event that happened in the past. The site of the Tenth was still just land back in the 1800s, but people surely walked up and down the unpaved and uncultured land. Perhaps a significant event that had a lot of emotional impact occurred, such as a proposal, a break up, or something else that would generate the immense amount of energy needed to create an imprint.

Then my thoughts were interrupted by footsteps on the floor above us. I then radioed Jay and asked him for his current location.

"On the roof," he replied.

I then asked him to count everyone in his group to make sure that everyone was accounted for.

"Yep, everyone is here," he said.

So everyone was accounted for, and there was a floor in between us. The footsteps felt like heavy boots.

"Can you move your feet faster?" I asked the unseen presence.

The stomps increased in speed.

Well, then. At this point I was getting a bit anxious. I was experiencing intelligent responses, even more so than during my very first investigation at the Tenth.

I then decided to tell the group what my team experienced on our first trip to the Tenth with the footsteps. I got up to demonstrate where each team member was sitting when we heard them. As I walked around the circle of people in the middle of the floor to show where I was sitting, I suddenly felt a firm hand grab the backside of my thigh.

I let out a loud shriek, and looked over at the circle of people about ten feet away who looked at me with confused faces.

This photo was taken right before my leg was grabbed.
Courtesy of Ann Ryan.

"Who just grabbed me?" I asked accusingly. I didn't appreciate getting grabbed by another person.

"No one grabbed you," David replied.

"Bull. Someone's hand grabbed the back of my leg and—"

My leg got grabbed again. I let out another shriek.

This time I was looking straight at my party, and the person closest to me was too far to actually touch me, let alone get back to their original position by the time I turned around. I've been doing this for a while. I've investigated for ten years, and never in my life had I ever experienced being grabbed like that. I had been on well over fifty investigations, everything from solo ghost hunts, team investigations, and paid ghost hunting tours. I've always had the light brushing or tingling sensation that could easily have been biological responses to my anxiety and changes in the environment. This was a full-on grab. If I didn't know any better, I would say that someone actually grabbed my thigh to keep me from walking someplace that could cause me harm. Two members of my group got up and investigated the area as I was trying to calm down. When it comes to getting grabbed, you also feel like it's a violation of your personal space. While looking back now, I appreciate getting grabbed because it reinforced my beliefs about the building being haunted. There was probably no better way to get my attention than literally grabbing my right leg to say, "Hey, I'm here! Pay attention to me!"

This photo was taken shortly after the leg-grab incident. Ann took a photo of the empty room and captured this. Courtesy of Ann Ryan.

As my group was helping me come back down from the emotional high, another member of the group asked if he could pull out his flashlight as a method of communication. I looked at him with a face that probably expressed, *Are you kidding me?* I've always been very skeptical over the flashlight method of communication because I feel like the person asking questions can heavily manipulate it—especially if they put the flashlight in front of them on a table. They could use their body to make the flashlight turn on and off if the attachment is sensitive. After explaining my concerns, I told the person that they were certainly more than welcome to try it, but the result could lead to false positives and misleading information. So, they placed the flashlight on the concrete floor and gave themselves a good distance away from the flashlight and started to ask questions.

"Can you turn the flashlight on?" he asked.

Flashlight instantly turns on.

"Okay, now turn it off," I said.

The flashlight remained on. Clearly, this person wanted more distinct instructions.

"If you are the Victorian woman, turn the flashlight off," I said.

Then there was nothing for several seconds. As we approached the minute mark, I decided I wasn't asking the right questions. So, then I ask, "If you were the entity that touched me, turn the flashlight off."

The flashlight turns off. I then tell the group to pause the questioning for several minutes because I wanted to see if the flashlight was being faulty and just turning on and off at random intervals. For several minutes we stare at the flashlight as it remained off. I then tell the group to move around and see if they can turn the flashlight on with their body. There is still nothing.

"Okay, now turn the flashlight on."

The flashlight turns on. At this point, I'm actually a bit irritated because I had just delivered this soapbox rant about how the flashlight method was ineffective, but now it was even surprising me with communication efficiency. Then, the same gentleman who had asked to use the flashlight in the first place asked another question.

"Do you like Alex? If so, turn the flashlight off."

A few seconds go by, and I'm thinking, oh great, the ghosts don't even like me. But then the flashlight turned off. Whew ... glad to know I'm liked by unseen entities.

At this point, Jay radios in.

"Hey Alex, can we switch places now?"

I hadn't realized that we had been in there for almost forty-five minutes when we were supposed to rotate about every twenty minutes. I radioed Jay to tell him that switching is fine, and I told the group that our time in the writing room on the third floor was done.

As the two groups were coming together, I asked Jay if anything significant happened on the roof. He said that it was pretty quiet up there, so I decided that I would take the group down to the basement/wine cellar. I didn't want to take my group to the roof if there wasn't going to be much activity, and I didn't want to disturb Jay's group by walking up and down the stairs several times, so I made the executive decision to move the group underground. With this, there would be two empty floors in between us, reducing the possibility of false positives from footsteps or extra noise. Jay also said that he would let me know when they moved to the Fourth-Floor Theater.

As we headed down to the basement, I commented that we're right near the staircase where Missy reportedly died and that she can sometimes be seen peering around the corners, but once you get around, there is no one there. The group nervously giggled, and I noticed that they get a little closer to each other and push me to the front of the pack. I'm thinking that after the events in the writing room, they were probably anticipating a bloodied girl standing in the middle of the empty hallway screaming at them. As we approached the doorway to the cellar, I tell the group that the stairs are very steep, to the point to where it may as well be a ladder, and to be extremely careful going down. I had a group of about seven to ten people, and given that my small team was cozy in the basement before, they were probably going to feel like a can of sardines.

Returning to the Basement

Since our last visit, I saw that Jeff had cleared out space in the middle of the basement and added some wine racks to the wall, making it more spacious. I took a cozy spot in the corner, diagonal from the ladder, while the rest of the group formed a semicircle. The same gentleman who brought out the flashlight then brought out a toy. He mentioned that in case there was a child around, he wanted to use a trigger object. Rommel then said that he felt the presence of a little boy. At this point, I brought out my ghost box, which is essentially a broken radio that sweeps through the channels without being muted. It is believed that ghosts can communicate through these airwaves and make their voices heard. Several investigators have been conducting ongoing studies of the ghost box (also known as a spirit box), and the results have either been inconclusive or results were determined to be audial pareidolia. Which essentially means that the human mind is trying to make sense of nonsense by creating patterns that make sense. If you have ever stared at the clouds and began seeing faces or animals, this is basically the same thing. You will run into matrixing and pareidolia issues in the area of spirit photography where someone will believe they see something in the pixilated photos while getting into arguments with others who don't see anything at all.

I've had some interesting experiences with the ghost box to determine that I wanted to keep the tool in my equipment for future use. That's why I had it on hand when I decided to see if we could communicate with anything in the basement. First, I had the radio sweep through the AM channels, as it was usually filled with political radio stations and mainly had adult voices on their shows and commercials, so if a child were to come through, there was a better chance of hearing them. As my ghost box began to sweep through the stations, I opened with my usual speech of wanting to communicate and wanting to hear the stories from the other side.

Then, we heard a high-pitched voice of a child saying "Hello." Even in the faded light, I could see the heads of my group snap to the little sweeping radio. Then a woman in our group asked, "How old are you?"

And almost simultaneously, Rommel and the box said "Seven." I was sitting with skepticism, as I didn't want to lose my control like I did in the writing room. As the group continued to ask questions, it seemed as though the entity in the basement was a young boy who was related to Missy either as a sibling or maybe a distant relative. Of course, the only child that is reported to be haunting the Tenth is Missy. But I wasn't ready to give up on this child entity yet. I began to think of possible theories as to what may have been occurring if we were to assume that communication with the little boy was legitimate.

I've always wondered whether that state we revert to in the afterlife is our permanent state. Meaning, if I go back to my eighteen-year-old self after I die, am I stuck in that age, or can I revert back to various ages of my own choosing? Could it be possible that the little boy we were talking to had lived to a ripe old age, but once he died, he became like a child again? And maybe, if he was really a sibling of Missy, perhaps he missed her so much that his soul returned to the location where she died so that he could spend the rest of eternity with her. These theories were a stretch, but considering that there was an active interaction occurring with the ghost box, and a child's voice cutting through, this warranted further investigation.

As the group kept asking questions, meeting perfunc-tory one-word answers or nothing at all, I looked at the red ball that Michael had placed on the floor. I really wanted that ball to move on its own. I wanted to see something with my eyes right in front of me. I didn't want anything out of my peripheral vision, I wanted to witness something remarkable right before my eyes in front of witnesses so that there was no question as to what took place. Maybe I was asking for too much. Perhaps I was beginning to cross the line of treating the ghosts as if they were circus animals. I was beginning to feel guilty because I was doing the very thing that I had always spoken so vehemently against.

"Don't feel bad," mentioned Rommel. I swear it was almost like he was reading my mind.

"What?" I said in reply.

"They like the attention. You're approaching this with respect, and you're doing this as a way to get their voices heard. Don't feel bad," he said.

Perhaps the look on my face was enough to let Rommel know what was going on. I don't know. Maybe my thoughts were loud enough that his psyche was able to pick it up. Or maybe even the ghosts knew what was going on and they let Rommel know so he could pass on the message. Who knows? The interaction was freaky and didn't leave my mind for several months.

As the responses on the ghost box began to dwindle down, I told the group that it was time to wrap up and meet the rest of the group in the gallery since the first round of people were packing up to leave. As I said goodbye to the people departing, one woman by the name of Donna Malmborg pulled me aside. Donna is a paranormal investigator in the San Diego area and she was very well respected in the community for her approach as an objective investigator who always questions more than she believes.

"Can I talk to you?" she asked. She looked concerned.

An Unexpected Experience

I nodded and we both stepped outside. She told me about how Jay took the group up to the roof first, where they did some EVP sessions but weren't getting much in response. So, after the groups switched places, Jay took the group to the Forum Theater on the fourth floor. This particular room was where the team and myself had originally set up our headquarters during our first visit. Less than a year ago, that room was filled with random set pieces for filming, with a raised platform, which was the stage area. By the time this third visit had happened, there was now an area for an audience to sit, and the stage was now completely built with a wall and a backstage area.

Donna stated that she and two other women were conducting an EVP session on the stage when they kept seeing a shadow in the corner of their eyes and were feeling genuinely creeped out. Once Jay announced that it was time to go, Donna stayed behind to take in the area. Once she stepped from the inside of the room into the hallway, she heard a man's voice whisper. Upon hearing this, she went back into the theater, but heard nothing else. She then stepped into the hallway again, and the whispering occurred once more. Donna surveyed the area, and the men had already begun to make their way downstairs with the rest of the group, and Donna was alone on the fourth floor. One more time, she went back into the room, and once again stepped out—and heard the whisper one last time.

At this point, I asked her if she had her audio recorder on, which she said no. It's funny how that always works. You experience something remarkable and paranormal, but none of the devices are on. I find this happening on a regular basis even with the investigators who do this frequently. It seems that the ghosts always wait until the recording devices are off before making their appearance.

"So, what do you think you experienced?" I asked.

"Well, whatever it was, it wasn't human," she replied.

That statement was interesting to me. She meant that the sound wasn't from a living human, but for a moment I had considered that maybe she meant something inhuman. That would have opened a completely different can of worms. As I listened to Donna's story, I was in awe. Memories of our first visit to the Tenth were flooding back, and the frightful memory of that shadow crossing in front of the mirror repeatedly sent chills up my spine. Now, three people who had no knowledge of that experience were now telling me that they had the same experience. All I will say is that receiving validation is really nice.

At that point, Donna had to depart for the night since she had to work early the next morning. As the group gathered and took a break in the lobby, there was one more place that I wanted to take them. I wanted to take everyone into the gallery and do a Ganzfeld session. I figured, why not? I had enough people with me, and this would give the rest of the group extra time to explore the rest of the building.

This is the hallway where Donna heard a man's voice whisper.

Group Ganzfeld

The first people to go under the Ganzfeld were Michael and Rommel. As they got set up, the rest of the group was eagerly watching. I realized that I had never taken this group through this experiment before, so as we were setting up, I explained what each part of the experiment meant, and why we were using it.

"The white noise and the white glasses help with the sensory deprivation and gives the mind a clean slate to work with, and the red light is a color that relaxes you but not enough to make you fall asleep," I said.

As the men were beginning the experiment, I told them to tell me what they were seeing. Rommel was instantly getting images of a bustling town from the 1800s with women in dresses and men in suits. Michael was getting the same imagery. I had Gus taking notes, and when we compared what each person heard afterward, there was some remarkable similarities. It seems as though Michael and Rommel were getting a picture of what life was like back during the time the First Baptist Church was first built. There were no negative experiences, and overall very pleasant as the rest of the willing group members volunteered to go under the Ganzfeld. Evidence-wise, there wasn't anything groundbreaking, but the group had a good time, and that was what mattered to me.

As the rest of the group departed the building, I looked at Jay and we both smiled. After a frustrating second trip to the Tenth, this recent trip made up for it. There were scares and laughs, and I got the reassurance that yes, there was something there at the Tenth—and it wasn't just my imagination.

Sadly, this also marked the last time that Jay and I would be at the Tenth for a long time, and the last time the original APS team would be together as a whole before we all went our separate ways.

Eight

EXPLANATIONS AND THEORIES

Whether anyone believes that there is anything paranormal at the Tenth Avenue Arts Center or not, I've come to regard the deceased people there as my friends. Whether it's Missy, the Pastor, or the British Lieutenant, I feel like they are there, choosing to remain in the Tenth as everlasting watchers over the building until it no longer stands. What started as a space where I was able to be an actor, a writer, an audience member, and a paranormal investigator has become a place other people are intrigued by as they discover that there is more to the Tenth than meets the eye. It may sound weird to consider a bunch of ghosts as friends, but given how many times I've been to the Tenth and have consistently acknowledged them with each visit, the dynamic is difficult to describe. During my time there, I felt I've become an accepted presence in the environment. Did I earn the respect of the ghosts? I try not to think of it that way, since I feel it is a bit selfish and egotistical, but I definitely feel like they know me in some way.

A Lost Child

One of the most common questions I've been asked not only by investigators but also from people who frequent the Tenth has been this: why is Missy the way she is? Well, when you're a young child like her, and you've been given nearly free rein of the space, what would you do? If the girl I found is the Missy haunting the Tenth, she died at the young age of ten years old. She was about six months away from turning eleven, which, if we think in terms of size and attitude, means she was probably getting ready to start the fifth grade. With this in mind, her maturity level could have been anywhere from still being like a little kid to trying to act like a young woman. From the testimony of Rommel, his reading of her was that she was mischievous and likes to get a reaction out of the people who are in the building whether they are looking for ghosts or not.

I can't verify what happens to us after we die, but in the event that our consciousness does survive in another state as a ghost, spirit, or some other form, and if there is a destination after death that is met by going through the light, would we go right away? Rommel stated that the ghosts that are present in the building are choosing to stay put instead of moving on. Of course, this is all conjecture and based on hypothetical scenarios, but I invite you to entertain me with your thoughts on this.

Going back to the original question with some more details, why would Missy choose to stay put instead of moving on to the light? A child who is innocent choosing to stick around instead of moving on to the next realm is a fascinating topic in itself. Perhaps she enjoys being in the world of the living or is trying to live vicariously through the living because her life was cut so short. I don't know.

The other thought is that perhaps Missy has moved on to the light, but she comes back to her old stomping grounds where she spent a lot of time. There are theories that explore the possibility that once one moves on to the light, they are able to come back whenever they please. Do I have proof of this occurring? The answer is no. But of all paranormal theories, the vast majority have not been proven. It can be a frustrating field because not everyone will be on the same page or agree with each other, which leads to a lot of fighting and bickering within the community. And as stated numerous times, there technically is no scientific proof to support the idea that ghosts even exist. So how can the paranormal field even come to a consensus as to what theories are right and wrong?

Returning to the Missy debate: My personal attempts at trying to find more about Missy's family came to several dead ends. Even just knowing that these stories are gradually becoming more lost as time progresses is sad. I know it's because institutions are still respecting the family's privacy, which is just fine.

Some stories aren't meant to be told. However, I believe that the stories that were told to Jeff have some element of truth to them—otherwise, where did they come from? The church would have a lot to lose if they ended up being true, and Jeff would have something to lose by making this stuff up himself. I believe that each myth and urban legend holds some sort of truth. With the congregation of the First Baptist Church being in the thousands, there was more than one pastor to help preside over the congregation. And do we have information on every person who ever walked through the doors of the church or even the chapel? No. And it will take years to finally figure it out. Besides old newspaper clippings of such as birth announcements, obituaries, and weddings, there's not a lot of information to go on as to who attended the church.

Brick Walls Can Be Beautiful

Historical research also sheds some light on the fact that there isn't a record of a Baptist Pastor committing suicide in the building. Granted, I believe that Jeff was being genuine in his testimony and that the First Baptist Church of San Diego really did convey the stories to him as they were moving out of the building. Given the timeline of the events that were said to have occurred there, and the age of the people who spoke to Jeff, could they have been the same people who were around at the time of Missy's death or the Pastor's suicide? If anything, they would be second-generation family members who might have heard about the incidents from parents, or even their grandparents. San Diego by nature is a city mixed with people who live and die there, along with people who live there and then move on to another place. Given that the church has been relatively unresponsive to inquiries, I suppose that will remain a mystery. Lack of historical support aside, when people have paranormal experiences, we have to keep looking for the evidence, regardless of brick walls.

Now, this only delves into the theory that the ghosts present in the building have some sort of connection to the space and are therefore bound to it. What if the ghosts who are there aren't even associated with the building at all? Some paranormal theories assert that ghosts attach themselves to objects such as toys, clothing, or jewelry. If this is the case, because the Tenth is a theater that hosts numerous productions, you can bet that many of the companies that rent the space also rent their set and costume pieces. So is it possible that perhaps maybe one or two of these ghosts came in on a rented object and then decided to stick around long after the production ended? Or what if the attachment came through via another person? Since we are talking about paranormal phenomenon that seems to not follow a set standard of rules, it might be possible.

Whether or not historical research lines up with present-day activity, there is no question that something weird is going on at the Tenth that's worth investigating. The nature of the unknown is to remain unknown, so would it really ever be that easy to be able to open and close the case of the Tenth? Of course not. But with the overwhelming eyewitness accounts, plus the investigators that I have worked with who have confirmed that the location is haunted, and the corresponding stories of the experiences that were had, there is something more going on. The only proof I have to offer you in terms of whether the Tenth is haunted is eyewitness testimony. Out of all the people that were spoken to and interviewed, all of them believe that the Tenth is haunted. Interpretations of the haunting will vary from person to person, but there is a consensus that there is something strange going on behind the doors. I can tell you that the paranormal community and the theater community in San Diego were separate for the longest time—even with me being around as that bridge between the two worlds, there isn't much to indicate that ghost hunters and actors are getting a beer together on Friday nights. So, when there is testimony from witnesses who don't have connections to each other, but remain consistent, what does that tell us?

I'm also quite certain that my team or any other team that has investigated the Tenth recently will not be the last group to go into the building. I'll remain a firm believer in the fact that publicly haunted locations warrant multiple investigations. The Tenth is certainly no exception, especially given that we have had different experiences with each visit. Sometimes the investigation will be a bust, but sometimes you may get something that is truly a head scratcher.

In the times that I've been at the Tenth as an actor, playwright, or audience member, I found myself talking to the empty space. Maybe it was to satisfy the loneliness and general weirdness of being in a building by yourself. But I always felt as though someone was there listening intently. The energy of the space would shift as if responding to the dynamics of the environment. Maybe the building itself is just alive?

Who knows? I just hope that the teams that go in there treat the space with respect for what it is. It is a theater that also hosts several businesses. Also, I hope people respect the space as a former religious institution. With this in mind, the Tenth has a history of spirituality not bound to one faith. Of course, from its inception until about 1997, the building was a church that worshiped Jesus Christ. But now, the Tenth is a building that celebrates and worships the creativity that man can bestow upon society. And that alone is enough to respect the space. Even if you don't believe the building is haunted, still respect the building.

If you do believe that there are ghosts at the Tenth, then you need to respect the ghosts. Depending on your religious background, the overall general belief is that ghosts used to be people who were alive. They had stories to share and experiences that made them human. Just because they are missing their physical body doesn't make them worth any less than you or I who are alive right now. From research and just hearing stories in general, I've found that the majority of people who have a negative experience investigating a haunted space weren't respecting the space or the people who work and live there.

The Decorum of Ghosts

While we are on the point of religion and how it influences the way we treat entities in the paranormal, I will say that since becoming an investigator, I have become much more open-minded when it comes to different religions. At the end of the day, it is all about faith. I have seen cleansing rites and prayers from other religions that have resolved cases just as effectively as someone using the name of Jesus. If we consider the possibility that maybe our religious texts aren't 100 percent right or really accept the fact that the book was written by man, then perhaps the verses about ghosts might be wrong. If we get that point across to the ghost hunters who throw the Bible around like it is bug spray, then maybe we will take a step forward in terms of showing more respect for the spirits of those who have passed on. The ghosts of the Tenth are no exception to that mind-set.

Think about it: if someone were to walk into your home and start cussing and shouting at you demanding that you prove yourself, how would you react? You probably wouldn't react very positively and instead be very short and mean in order to protect yourself and your space. When APS made the first trip to the Tenth and experienced the negative presence in the Fourth-Floor Theater, we could have responded similarly to it, and thus, created an exchange of negativity. Where would that have gotten us? At the same time, I don't believe that we should ever allow ourselves to be pushed around or bullied by those on the other side. I have to commend

Beverly because when she felt the presence of a ghost in her face, she was calm but firm when she told it to get out of her face. It wasn't disrespectful; it simply sent the message that she didn't want to be messed with and that she had a job to do: establish communication and connect with the ghosts in the building. If you go into any haunted space with neutrality and respect, you're generally going to get a more productive response from the environment and from the presences that dwell there. While the Tenth initially began as an investigation of experiences in order to confirm if something was really going on, it has morphed into an ongoing research project. In the end, all of our investigations should be that way, even the fun ones in haunted places. And I think that if you go into a haunting with that genuine desire, the ghosts will be more than willing to go along with it.

The main value of an ongoing research project such as the one at the Tenth is that it increased the chance of finding corroborating evidence under different circumstances. For example, the ghosts at the Tenth are very familiar with my team, which is great, but has its limits. We can gain more insights by comparing notes after an investigation by someone who has not spent a significant amount of time at the Tenth. This was the case when Donna and her group saw a shadow on the stage and heard the whispers every time she tried to leave the room.

Considering that she had never heard details about our experience and only had general knowledge that the building was haunted, it is remarkable that she would have a similar experience. Given that I know how Donna will question everything to the point of making you feel like a fool at the end of the conversation because she will always bring up theories and logical explanations, I trust her findings.

Granted, many people have access to the Internet nowadays, and I can only speak for my own psychic mediums that went into the space cold with little to no information. I can only speak of supervising several psychic mediums in the building at the same time who all picked up similar phenomenon. If someone is going to debunk the haunting and the experiences at the Tenth, I welcome their explanations that can actually be supported from spending a significant amount of time in the theater rather than from secondhand sources or making judgments after just one visit. This is because after several visits, while I feel closer to answering the questions, I'm still not confident in my answers.

Until it can be explained, I continue to picture the ghosts of the Tenth roaming the halls and peering through the windows and observing the world of the living. I believe they are in a state of limbo or purgatory. Should someone choose to engage with them, whether the ghosts respond is up to them. While they have engaged in conversation and interacted, based on my team's second trip to the Tenth, which resulted in zero interactions, it is clear that they do so on their own terms—and no one else's. If they don't want to talk to you, you won't get a response. If they are in the mood, they will not only interact with you, you just might get more than you bargained for, and even get grabbed! I also think that you have to approach the ghosts from a perspective of respect and curiosity. Know their story before going in and try to engage them based on that information. To give you the shortened explanation, once you go in, talk to them like they are your friends, and they will be there to talk back to you. I still found myself giving a nod to the ghosts of the Tenth whenever I was in the building even when I wasn't there as a paranormal investigator.

What if we approached every haunting with the research and background knowledge already put in place and talk to the deceased as if they were the people they once were? Perhaps there will be less aggression in paranormal interactions and more productive conversations. Once those conversations happen, and they are documented, maybe we will become closer to an answer as to what happens after we die. The ghosts at the Tenth hold the answers of what awaits us after we die, and maybe it is time to listen. I often feel conflicted by my own actions in the space, as I spent too much time trying to get the experience of talking to the ghosts at the Tenth, but I didn't spend a lot of time actually listening to what they had to say.

The next time I'm in San Diego, you bet I will be at the Tenth Avenue Arts Center on another investigation. This time, I'll be there just to listen without the expectation from the ghosts to perform tricks. I want to just sit in the main stage area and say, "Talk to me. I'm here to listen." Because I've hit dead ends in the historical research, perhaps the ghosts can tell me something about themselves that will point me in the right direction toward finding the proper historical evidence of their existence. One of the things that frightens me the most about death is the fact that once I die, my story will be gone for good. The ghosts at the Tenth don't have a life story right now. But it is out there somewhere, in a dusty drawer at a library or on a headstone in a cemetery. There is a lead somewhere out there that will take me to the moment where I can verify Missy's existence and bring some clarity to the Pastor who committed suicide by giving him a name.

I feel like that is something that I owe my friends at the Tenth. They have given so much to me in terms of growing my knowledge and experience in the field, the least I can do is give them a real name and a face that has been forgotten for so long.

———————

I wanted to dedicate some time to discuss some possible explanations of the phenomenon at the Tenth Avenue Arts Center, both logically and paranormally. It is important to know that while there were numerous eyewitness accounts of the phenomenon at the Tenth, there has to be an effort to keep the book balanced. I don't want you to think that I just walk around and call everything I see a ghost or some form of paranormal activity. Looking at the Tenth from both sides will make your experience with this book well-rounded and ultimately, leave the decision up to you, the reader, as to what is going on in the old building. For me to simply declare the ghosts of the Tenth as formerly living souls who chose to hang out in the old building as part of their final resting place would be an extraordinarily ignorant decision on my part and make me an unreliable source—not only in investigating the Tenth, but also for paranormal research as a whole. Of course I have seeds of doubt in the back of my mind too as I entertain the possibility that the ghosts don't exist at all, and the occurrences and experiences we had were just emulating a circus. Whether these explanations make sense to you will heavily depend on your experience and knowledge of the paranormal, as well as how open your mind is to different possibilities.

Let us start with the logical explanations first, and then work our way to the extraordinary explanations.

First of all, there is a lot of outside noise at the Tenth in the stairways and the hallways. Even in the writing room you can hear cars and trucks outside, and if someone is substantially loud, you can hear their entire side of the conversation. At first, it could be discouraging and one could easily throw out the potential of ever being able to capture good audio evidence. However, when it came to the "Mommy" that Jay heard, while that sound was captured on multiple recording devices, the word sounded like it was being said in the presence of the guys. It was not faint nor did it have an echo-like sound as if the voices were from the outside. But outside noise is crucial to consider in the reported experiences at the Tenth, and it is important to know the difference between a voice coming from within the building and a voice coming from someone walking down the sidewalk outside. The reason why I know this? We tagged our audio recording. Even if someone whispered, sneezed, or there was a bug squeaking around inside the room, we tagged it by describing what the sound was. Because of the amount of outside noise coming through, we were able to differentiate what sounds were coming from outside or inside from their tone and wavelengths on the computer. If you don't tag your audio recording, you will run into false positives as well as have a number of unexplainable sounds. If you don't make it a habit to tag, you will not be able to distinguish sounds that are potentially from the other side from sounds that have a logical explanation. I will admit that the investigations at the Tenth literally forced my team to learn basic sound engineering so we could analyze any audio.

The next thing to consider while attempting to analyze and explain the phenomenon are the footsteps that sounded like they were coming from the floor above. The floors and ceilings at the Tenth are completely made of cement. Now, of course, I wasn't physically there when the building was built, but it's also safe to assume that there are pipes and various kinds of spacing in between the slabs of concrete that make up the sturdiness of the building. Realizing this, we have to consider the possibility that rodents can get in between those spaces and make copious amounts of noise. Of course, the continuous thumping of footsteps can sound a bit different from a rat scurrying between the spaces. And the noise that we heard above us really sounded like someone with boots stomping in the room above. Paranormal? Maybe, maybe not. But we have to consider these possibilities and apply them to our problem-solving skills while we are in the midst of the investigation and try not to get too caught up with the experience of the phenomenon.

Now it is time to switch gears to purely parapsychological explanations, which is part of the other debate about the Tenth since there isn't much in regard to historical records to support the haunting. The key question here is: What if the ghosts that are present aren't even ghosts of deceased people, but instead, manifestations of our minds?

In various forms of Buddhism, there is a powerful practice of meditation that encompasses in the creation of something called a *tulpa* or "thought form," or creating an entity of their own. It takes an immense amount of discipline and practice in order to master this technique. Tulpas and thought forms have come up in Indian Buddhism as well as Tibetan Buddhism. Alexandra David-Neel became one of the first researchers to observe this practice during her study in Tibet in the early twentieth century. In her studies, she also noted that with enough dedication and attention, the tulpa could eventually create a mind of its own and become free from its maker. While researchers and scholars have debated as to whether tulpas are merely hallucinations, Buddhist monks believe that tulpas are deities. This sort of practice takes years of strict discipline and teaching through meditation, and it has been a phenomenon that fascinates the Western world. David-Neel was a spiritual person, and she herself engaged in the practice of creating a tulpa, which she created in the image of Friar Tuck. In her diaries, she noted that the tulpa had created a mind of its own, which subsequently forced her to destroy it. What also caught my attention was the fact that tulpas and thought forms have been linked to imaginary friends, and there are websites dedicated to helping people create their own tulpas to relieve their loneliness.

Natural Recordings

Earlier in this book, I briefly spoke about the Stone Tape Theory. Jumping on the same theory of how tulpas are created, the same could be said for the Stone Tape Theory. If the mind is powerful enough to create its own entity, then it isn't too much of a reach to say that the same energy could be created and then left to fester and grow in the surrounding environment of inanimate objects. This means that the walls, the chairs, the building, the sets, costumes, props, etc., are recording moments in time that entail a great amount of emotional energy.

Because numerous psychics picked up on the death of Missy and the Pastor, perhaps these psychics were sensing the residual energy that was left behind from the emotionally traumatic experience. This is a plausible scenario that is supported by the theories of Dr. William G. Roll, whose studies assert the possibility that we all have "psi fields," carriers of information that is then relayed to our minds. This goes along with the theory that ghosts are not actual physical manifestations, but instead, they are manifestations of the mind. This could very well be the reason why it is so difficult to capture an image of a ghost but we can still see and hear them. Of course, the outsider and disbeliever reading this may interpret this theory as me saying that it is all in our minds. But if Roll was right and we are carriers of psi fields, then this says a lot about the survival of our consciousness and how we are able to communicate with the world of the dead. These psi fields collect information from the external environment and pass it on to our brains, which then communicate to our bodies (such as feeling like we're being touched or experiencing a drop in temperature).

Let us return to the area of tulpas and thought forms for a moment.

In the 1970s, a group of Canadian parapsychological researchers engaged in an experiment of creating their own ghost. The purpose behind the experiment was to prove that the human mind could not only create its own ghost, but also produce its own paranormal activity. This experiment started out with sessions of long concentration, focusing on the ghost that they named "Philip Aylesford," and they gave him an entire backstory, including a tragic demise. The sessions only consisted of concentration, with no contact or speaking to Philip. Then the group transitioned to a spiritualism-style séance and began to initiate contact with Philip. At first, he only manifested in the form of rappings, but as the sessions continued, he began to get stronger. He answered questions about his life and exhibited historically accurate information that wasn't a part of the first half of the experiment. The group of researchers concluded that perhaps this information came from their own minds and was transferred in the process of giving Philip his backstory. Philip was able to slide the table around and move objects even though he never manifested as an apparition. Along with the conscious action of creating a ghost of your own, the people who participated in the experiment didn't count on the unconscious exchange of information that took place. With this in mind, we have to wonder how much control do we really have over what exactly our minds can do? We can go in with good intentions, but it seems that our own imaginations can run away from us and create something that was much more than what we intended.

Creating Our Own Ghosts

The Philip Experiment is interesting to take into account when it comes to the Tenth Avenue Arts Center. Perhaps the people who told Jeff the stories of Missy, the Pastor, and the British Lieutenant had heard the legends or myths when they were significantly younger, and subsequently, over time (along with others who knew of the story) continued to feed their energy into these entities, thus gaining their own identity and form of "life." After the story was passed on to Jeff, it could be possible that these three entities then survived from Jeff's consciousness as well as that of whoever he spoke to about the ghosts at the Tenth. This could explain why paranormal activity is taking place at the building regardless of the lack of historical evidence. The very idea that we can create our own ghosts is terrifying just by itself, especially since there are some very disturbing people out there whose minds I never want to visit. In that case, what if the entire paranormal investigation field was dealing with the manifestations of our minds? No wonder it can be so disturbing and terrifying sometimes.

Now, if we are going to take the tulpa theory, plus the occurrences of the Philip Experiment into consideration, let's go further with the hypothesis that the three main ghosts are thought forms. Tulpas exist and survive based on energy. While it is unclear as to what type of energy they need to survive, we can safely assume that theaters are hubs for energy, both electrical and physical. When theatrical productions take place, there are lights, sounds, microphones, and lots of plugs, computers, soundboards, and other various forms of electrical equipment. Given the amount of high EMF (electromagnetic fields) being emitted from the equipment, it could also be possible that people are experiencing EMF poisoning, which can result in experiencing paranormal-like hallucination. High EMF has been associated with paranormal activity for years and has become almost mainstream knowledge since the inception of reality television shows about ghost hunting. While there isn't solid proof that ghosts emit or absorb EMF, there is an association with high EMF levels and paranormal activity, which is likely linked to the person experiencing the phenomenon.

Along with the energy from EMF, we also have physical and mental energy coming from the cast and crew of the various theater companies that use the Tenth for their productions. It's a wonder to consider a theory that involves actors creating their own tulpas and manifestations based on the characters they are playing. Depending on the intensity of the actor, could it be possible that in their process of getting into character, they created a thought form, free to roam the earth long after the production is over? It's a stretch, but considering we're talking about the paranormal here, nothing is too far of a stretch for the believer and non-skeptic. From personal experience, while I am creating a character as an actor, I take elements of me and form them into an alternate version of myself to help me better present the character with an element of truth.

The Exchange of Energy

But even if actors aren't creating tulpas, they are still emitting energy in both their process of creating their character as well as in the performance. There is an exchange of energy between the actor and the audience. The audience produces its own energy by emotionally responding to the actors' performances, giving their energy to the actors and while receiving energy from the performers, making it into a continuous cycle of energy exchange. If you have ever been on a stage, you probably have an idea of what it's like to have a good audience—one that is responsive and basically making your performance feel like a success. And, when I say performance, I don't just mean donning a costume and saying lines on a stage with a set. Performance can mean anything from a public speaking event to presenting a project in front of colleagues.

So with this immense exchange of energy taking place, there is a response from the external environment. Ever walked into a room where two people just had a fight and the vibe of the room feels off? You can cut the tension in the room with a knife. This is a similar concept. Perhaps it isn't too big a leap to speculate that maybe the continuous energy bandied about between the performers and the audience could affect the entities that dwell within the Tenth.

Not to mention that there is also a decent amount of stored energy being introduced into the environment from costumes, props, and set pieces, which falls in line with the Stone Tape Theory. Sometimes well over dozens of people have worn the same dress or used the same props for hundreds of productions. With the belief that objects can be haunted, would it be crazy to theorize that maybe some of the ghosts of the Tenth possibly traveled by costume or prop? With all of the subconscious energy stored up, it is a wonder that there has not been more dramatic paranormal activity in the Tenth. But you also don't see actors or technicians going through a cleansing ritual with each new costume or prop that they receive.

Now, if the ghosts at the Tenth did indeed exist in the world of the living for a time, and they are ghosts or spirits, they are in the perfect place for not only energy, but also an entertaining place to be overall. Since numerous psychics have stated that the ghosts of the Tenth are there by choice and not bound to the land, why do they stay? With so many wondrous sights around the world, why settle for the Tenth Avenue Arts Center in San Diego, California? For anyone who has known me for a significant amount of time, I always ask who wrote the rules of the paranormal. Where does it say in what official rulebook that ghosts have to listen to us at all? Especially when we're establishing boundaries? I have a hard time accepting that a mischievous ghost will listen to my boundaries, let alone abide by them. But if the human mind really is as powerful as I've discussed, then perhaps it is we who create the rules for the other side, and we unconsciously set those boundaries on our own.

Well, I guess that is one of the numerous questions about the unknown that will likely remain unknown, but we can venture some theories. First, as just previously discussed, theaters are rich with energy. They are also places of entertainment. If these ghosts are anything like they were in life, then they probably want to be entertained and participate in an activity that they probably enjoyed in life. Also, theater is a mirror to society and a reflection of living the human experience. Perhaps the ghosts of the Tenth choose to stick around because the shows being produced, plus the building buzzing with people each day from the offices, at the Tenth are a reflection of the living world that the ghosts used to be a part of… and they miss that. The human experience is what we are experiencing right now. Once we are deceased and our physical bodies no longer exist, we live a different sort of existence. It is no longer human, but instead, spiritual.

The Ongoing Investigators

For the circumstances of the Tenth, since Jeff invites numerous teams into the building to investigate, I firmly believe that paranormal investigation is also a part of the human experience because we will all eventually experience death. Paranormal investigating and ghost hunting is the action seeking some sort of proof that there is life after death, and just having confirmation that it doesn't end once our physical bodies shut down is a comforting thought. The idea that our deceased loved ones aren't too far away means that they are not gone for good and that we will see them again eventually. For thousands of years, religion has attempted to answer the questions about the afterlife. From the ancient Egyptians to the ancient Greeks, the afterlife plays a prominent role in our society. In our contemporary society, with the rise of the digital age, even with religion as packed into our world as it is, our souls seem to be more lost than ever. As we watch our friends and family die, and reach a new chapter in their existence, we remain in the living world like lost lambs. I feel as though the desire to find proof of life after death during such times of despair is a major reason why people matrix photos and videos so much. So, in turn, the Tenth Avenue Arts Center is host to two major components of the human experience: the experience of living life, and the experience of dying.

But perhaps paranormal experiences aren't meant to be shared. Perhaps the supernatural world selects certain people to experience the unknown as a way to teach a lesson or give a warning about their current path. This could be the reason why when one person has an unexplainable experience, the phenomenon doesn't happen again and the experience cannot be verified. Could this be why there is so much discord in the paranormal community—because we are making public the experiences that are meant to be private? Will everyone believe that the Tenth is haunted? Of course not. I could probably show anyone photos of the ghosts, even after going through my own debunking process as a photographer, and not everyone will believe me. I can show off multiple recording devices that captured the voice saying "Mommy" to Jay and Rick, but not everyone will believe it. Knowing this, it is logical to ask what is the point of this book, and why even bother trying to explore the phenomenon at the Tenth?

It is all a matter of personal experience and what you as a human being want to get out of your exploration into afterlife studies. In this world, you have to be confident in your work and what you believe in; otherwise, those who oppose you will eat you alive. If I took it personally every time someone in this field was rude to me or tried to debunk something I witnessed firsthand, I would have never written this book. I have to hold firm to what I believe in and know that I have a story to tell.

There are many possible explanations that can either support or debunk the haunting at the Tenth Avenue Arts Center. From tulpas and energy imprints to logical explanations related to the construction of the building, it means so much more to me than just a haunted theater. The building itself has become a symbol for me as the melding of two passions in my life that seamlessly work together. It is the representation of seeking answers to what makes us human and how we can change the world, as well as representing the fear that I have when it comes to death. If Missy can give me some sort of reassurance that she is not only real, but that the journey of death means that there is some sort of consciousness after our physical bodies stop working, then I will be successful in my quest and study of the building on the corner of Tenth and E.

Nine

A DREAM REALIZED

After Jay, Beverly, and I moved away from San Diego to various parts of the East Coast, David took the reins of the team and became the director. Gus was still on the team, but not as active as before because he decided to go back to school. Since there was going to be a major gap in the team, I interviewed potential members from a distance and brought on Josh and Karen. They both displayed a level of passion for the paranormal that reminded me a lot of the working dynamic between Jay and me. Not to mention that Josh was also in the military. Rick and Jay had officially retired right before this, so the tradition of APS being a team with military connections remained.

And with that, that sealed the membership of these two newcomers. Karen took on the role of the caseworker, which was a job originally shared between Beverly and me, and she proved to be the ideal person for the job. She originally knew David first through their psychic Meetup group where people with abilities gathered in San Diego to work on their gifts. She was still developing her gift, and was completely okay with David remaining as the main psychic. I met Josh through our team recruitment online and fate that brought him our way. Even though there was a departure of three key team members, fate still took care of the team and made sure that those gaps were filled quickly.

When Jeff and I first started talking about the Tenth as a potential place for investigating, Jeff discussed his dream of having the building be a place where people could go on a haunted tour and experience the unknown firsthand. Originally, the goal seemed like a stretch, and he wanted to make sure there was something going on in the building from a team of knowledgeable investigators. With the Tenth celebrating Halloween with a bang, Jeff wanted to integrate the haunted tours with the month of October. This dream did not come to fruition while I was still in San Diego.

But it came true in 2014.

Finally, after all this time discussing, researching, and investigating, David and Karen were able to coordinate with Jeff on the haunted tours at the Tenth. This would be the first time in over a year that the general public would have access to the building for an investigation with the team. And I was confident that the ghosts of the Tenth would not disappoint.

Through e-mail correspondence, I advised Karen to do a preliminary investigation so that the new people like herself and Josh were already well acquainted with the space before taking members of the general public on the ghost tour.

To prepare for the tour, David and Karen did two preliminary investigations in the summer of 2014, bringing a fellow psychic named Shawn along so that there was another set of eyes on the case. During my follow-up call, Karen informed me that Shawn and David felt that sometimes the British Lieutenant attempts to block communication between the ghosts and the living. The motive is still uncertain as of the writing of this book, but it is certainly fun and interesting to consider. During my last investigation of the building a year before, Rommel noted that there was a man in the writing room who sometimes prevented Missy from communicating.

From their preliminary investigation, they were able to identify one more ghost at the Tenth, and she didn't have a name. When David, Karen, and Shawn (as a guest) investigated the Tenth, Shawn was drawn to a female energy in the writing room bathroom. He felt the woman was in her forties or fifties, and overall left a very weird feeling of energy in the space from her emotions while she was alive. When asked about it, Jeff realized who she was from a previous interaction with the volunteer who helped move the pipe organ out. But this corroboration was in an entirely different context. They weren't telling Jeff about the ghost stories; they were informing Jeff about a firsthand situation with the bathrooms, which is why the story didn't come to light until recently.

Carla

The fact that one of the ghosts has been recently identified shows that the study of the Tenth Avenue Theater is far from over. Her name is Carla, and it is believed that she occupies the writing room area. She was a prominent member of the First Baptist Church who was very active in the ministries offered and volunteered much of her time. But she also had a strange case of obsessive-compulsive disorder (better known as OCD). For example, if the church choir didn't fold their robes to her standards and specifications after the Sunday church service, then she would refold the robes. Carla was known for being socially awkward, and while some people didn't get along with her, she did good work for the church and was very dedicated.

During the seventies, the church went through some remodeling on the third and fourth floor (where the writing room, the gym, the art gallery, and the landing where Missy died is located). More bathrooms were added, but the workers and contractors didn't quite build the stalls to specifications. Instead of the doors opening outwardly, they opened inwardly, with the door hinges on the inside, causing some of the doors to hang backwards. This drove Carla crazy, and she even tried to get the workers to fix them, but they refused. She asked the pastor to fix the doors, but he declined because the church didn't want to spend any more money on the renovations. From that day on, Carla always complained about the bathroom doors, but she never saw them get fixed in her lifetime. When Jeff bought the building, he did fix the bathrooms so that the doors now swung correctly, but that doesn't seem like enough to keep Carla calm and at bay. Whatever is keeping Carla trapped in the Tenth (and in the bathroom of all places) seems to be enough of a burden to prevent her from moving on into the next phase of existence, such as heaven, hell, or another aspect of the afterlife.

The Portal

Also from the preliminary investigation, David and Shawn concluded that the writing room held some sort of portal in the space. In the paranormal world, a portal is an open door to the spirit world, meaning that things can step in and out at will. During my previous times at the Tenth, a portal had never been mentioned. This new information both alarmed and intrigued me. While a female energy was picked up at my last investigation, there wasn't as much detail as to identity. So, why did Carla choose to come out now? Did she come in through the portal? Why is the portal now becoming a topic of discussion?

Since learning of this new information, I began to compare case notes from the different visits. What I've noticed is that before the team took over as resident investigators, there were other investigators in the space. After I had moved, David was asked to investigate the Tenth with another team, so I was able to stay informed on their experiences. The results of their investigation suggested that the building was fairly quiet except for the knockings, rappings, and footsteps that we so often heard from previous investigations. From my conversation with Jeff, two other unnamed teams also visited the Tenth, but they did not share their results with him afterward. So, anything could have happened to have escalated the activity or brought Carla out from the darkness to communicate.

I had also noticed that the level of activity has risen, according to the reports by David, Karen, Josh, and Gus. I have started to ponder the idea that perhaps, somewhere down the line, someone may have opened up a vortex—whether it was an intentional decision or not is immaterial. If the portal has been there this whole time, it wasn't picked up by Rommel, David, Madison, or the first psychic that Jeff brought in before the investigations even started. So why now?

As mentioned before, the activity at the Tenth has seen an increase. Perhaps it is because of all the attention the space has received recently. If not the attention, then maybe the space has been manipulated in some way to either attract more ghosts or to rile up the ghosts who are currently residing in the Tenth. Either way, the recent escalation alarmed me. I wasn't sure if this was a good thing or something that could potentially require an intervention in the form of some sort of mediation or spirit rescue.

While I was still on the phone with Karen, I asked her if there have been any "extra" ghosts around the building and if they have picked up on anyone new that contradicts the past investigations. She mentioned to me that there are kids who now stop by the Tenth. A girl about the age of ten and a boy somewhere between age five and seven. Of course, this doesn't necessarily contradict past investigations because we had picked up on a young boy in the basement. Whether they are the same person, I can't confirm. And the young girl who is ten is not the same girl as Missy. Karen tried to rationalize why they hung out in the building.

She mentioned that they come by the Tenth because these kids know that there are people coming by who can see and hear them. This was a sound explanation, as I've learned that many times, all ghosts want to do is act like they're a living human again. The most basic trait that we all possess is communication, regardless if we are deaf or blind. We still have a way to communicate and our very spirit hungers for that interaction. If you were in a foreign country where no one spoke your language, the first thing you would do is seek out someone who could understand you.

I'm not an expert on the rules of the afterlife, but given my experience, I'm inclined to believe that ghosts aren't necessarily bound to one location. Of course, we must also consider the factor of variables since we run into the occasional case where a ghost is trapped someplace, caused by the living or the dead, though I'm not convinced that this restraint is universal. For example, numerous ghost hunters will shield and protect themselves during an investigation, and upon leaving, will command the ghosts to not follow them home or attach themselves to anyone.

The Vortex

David and Shawn also picked up a vortex in the writing room. This is not to be confused with the portal, which is essentially a doorway. A vortex is the twisting of energy, whether it's spiritual, magnetic, etc. In the paranormal sense, a vortex is the occurrence of several spirits spinning their energy together to make one energy. Sometimes this results in the ability to bend light, defy gravity, and literally twist objects around them (such as a plant). In some cases, a vortex can be powerful enough to create a portal. There are numerous vortices (plural for vortex) around the world, such as Stonehenge and the Pyramids of Egypt.

Vortices are also captured more often in photography. They will look like funnels of light in pictures and could often be mistaken for a person. If vortices have the energy to be able to manipulate light and create a presence that can reflect light, then it is entirely possible to entertain that theory. As a photographer, light is the central nervous system of photography. You can take great photos if you know how to manipulate light and use it to your advantage. This is why you see photographers carry around so much equipment from flashes to reflectors. In the case of the paranormal investigator, you often don't have a lot of light to work with, which often results in the weird photo with anomalies that can be debunked 90 percent of the time.

When in the presence of a vortex, people have reported feeling off, or unsettled. This would make sense if a vortex is truly the twisting of energy. This gave me a flashback to when

Beverly felt knotted up or twisted inside during her Ganzfeld session in the Fourth-Floor Theater, which also happens to be directly above the writing room. If vortices do exist, I don't believe that they are restricted to the boundaries of human architecture, so I would entertain the theory that the vortex from the writing room could be powerful enough to reach the next floor up.

Between the newly discovered information about Carla, the portal, and the vortex, a breath of fresh air was given to the investigations at the Tenth.

A Public Introduction

Flash forward to October of 2014, and the first tour was now underway for the general public. With Karen, David, and Josh ready to helm the evening, there was a decent turnout of about five to seven people per night. Given that the space is fairly small, instead of taking the groups apart, they all stayed together.

Karen first took the group to the door that leads to the basement. Upon entering, there is a door that takes you into a small room, and then a second door that takes you to a steep staircase that takes you into the basement. The second door was shut (and keep in mind that the floor is made out of cement). As Karen is introducing the basement, the second door began to shake and swung open, as if giving her an invitation to go in. This was enough to impress the attendees, and word began to spread about the haunting of the Tenth Avenue Theater. For the eight investigations that the team hosted, there was consistent activity that was identical to what we experienced in our previous investigations. The ghosts seemed to like their newfound attention.

The general public has maintained an interest in the space, and Jeff and I are constantly talking about ways we can present the Tenth to the public that is not only entertaining, but also educational. The Tenth has the ability to be an education hub for people who wish to learn more about the paranormal, and it is a relatively safe place to explore as long as you have a trained investigator with you. Investigating solo with little to no knowledge is not recommended, although I realize that it is how I learned to investigate and essentially figure out what to do and what not to do. If I had the chance to "try again," I would have loved to have had someone there to watch over me and tell me what I was doing right or wrong. So, here, the Tenth has an amazing potential to be that training ground for new investigators.

Escalation

Karen, Josh, and David returned to the Tenth in November for another investigation that was closed off from the public. At this particular investigation, they had some weird experiences that have given credence to the idea that there is something potentially darker inhabiting the space. The three started out on the rooftop, where they had an uneventful EVP session, so they decided to move back inside.

The team moved into the writing room. As they set up their EMF meters, they began to hear the footsteps from the floor above them (which, as mentioned before, would be the Fourth-Floor Theater). This time around they were able to clarify what kind of sound the footsteps were creating, comparing it to the sound of boots with a heavy heel. Karen, being the alert and constant debunker that she is, wanted to get to the bottom of the sound as it happened. As they went up the stairs, she passed the landing where Missy died, and noted that she felt extremely nervous and that there was a disturbed energy in the area. She called the other two guys to assist immediately several times before they finally reached her. Karen expressed that she was too nervous to be in the space but didn't want to leave it in case something else happened. She didn't want to risk losing out on the possibility to communicate further.

After David and Josh joined her, they sat on the landing. While doing so, the group began to feel a cold wind rush by them. Karen thought in the back of her mind that maybe the rooftop door was open.

But before she could even ask, David said, "I bolted the rooftop door as we were all inside."

At this point, the three began to hear footsteps from the floor above them. If they went up the next flight, they would be at the source of the sound. As they listened, the footsteps were dragging. And as the footsteps dragged, the windows on the office doors rattled, one by one. By this time, Karen was feeling a weird energy that was very similar to the writing room bathroom.

The group then decided to head down to the basement, where previously at the public tour, the door swung open by itself. In terms of equipment, they had two EMF meters (also known as K-2 meters) on hand. These meters track fluctuations in electromagnetic fields, which means that if you bring an electronic device near a meter, it will spike with lighted dots. EMF travels all around us, as it is emitted from our everyday electronics like computers and even electrical wiring. They brought the devices out and began their EVP session. Occasionally with EMF meters, there will be spikes from someone's walkie-talkie or cell phone. I had asked Karen if there were any devices nearby that could manipulate or taint the EMF meter reactions, and she said no.

While awaiting responses, the three began discussing the British Lieutenant, Missy, and the Baptist Pastor. There were no spikes on either of the meters. Then Karen asked:

"Are you a ghost of someone that we didn't mention?"

Immediately, both EMF meters began to spike. All of the colors were illuminated.

Josh noted to me that at this moment, he was shaken up. He had been on the team for almost a year by this point, and he had been on seven investigations. The reason I brought him onto the team was because of his ability to keep a level head and keep his cool. But at the moment that the EMF meters spiked, he felt a dark energy around him that felt as though it was up to no good. There was no other occurrence that would justify him feeling this unsettled.

When this occurs, oftentimes it is our own defense mechanisms kicking in, or our subconscious warning us that there is potential danger. When this happens, adrenaline begins to rush, goosebumps are formed, and the hair on the back of your neck stands up. It is your body getting ready to fight, and this really only happens in times of potential danger. Given that Josh was in the military and had been deployed before, this was a situation worth noting and investigating. Any time a team member with a military background responds to the environment like this, I pay closer attention. If anything, I trust their instincts and their judgment more than my own.

Josh excused himself and headed back to the lobby. As he went down the stairs and reached the lobby, the front doors slammed shut. Now, keep in mind that anytime APS has investigated the building, the front doors remained locked. This is done for team safety and to make sure that no equipment gets stolen. So for the front door to be open as Josh headed upstairs was bizarre, and for the doors to swing shut as fast as they did was not normal. Usually, only one door was open at a time, and never both at the same time. Josh rushed to open one of the doors, and as he looked outside, he saw no one—nothing but the balmy and foggy scene of the late San Diego night. He checked the door to the alleyway on the other side of the lobby, but it was locked and sealed. Why did the doors shut the way that they did? Were they trying to send a message saying that Josh wasn't allowed to leave yet?

Since Karen and Josh were the newest members of the team with the least amount of experience with the Tenth, I asked them if they felt that the theater was haunted.

I was met with a resounding, "Oh yes!"

Coming Full Circle

The dream and goal that seemed like it was so far away was now coming true. I will admit that I am sad that I don't get to be in San Diego to continue the ongoing study, but getting the reports from David, Karen, and Josh brings me so much joy. It is like putting together a puzzle where the pieces have been in different parts around the world, just waiting for someone passionate enough to gather them all together. And what makes this all even more beautiful is the fact that other people have joined in on the journey. From team members to members of the paranormal community, the Tenth Avenue Theater is becoming a hub where different minds can come together and discuss the phenomenon taking place.

The sheer fact that the team has become the go-to people to guide others through this haunted theater nearly brings tears to my eyes. All of the team members have grown so much, and the team itself has grown. If you were to have told me back in 2011 that this is what APS would become, I wouldn't have believed you. They are becoming respected members and experts in their own areas of focus, with different backgrounds and experiences. This dynamic, when brought together, is what I feel is making the tours at the

Tenth as successful as they are. What was once their training ground has become their laboratory for experimentation and discovering new and wondrous things about the Tenth and the ghosts who inhabit it.

CONCLUSION

Here we are ... we have reached the end of this journey. Revisiting my studies at the Tenth has made me literally ache in anticipation to return. This was unexpected, as the first time I entered the walls of the Tenth Avenue Arts Center, I never thought I would be writing a book about it. Even after the first couple of investigations, I didn't have a book in mind. But when summing up my case reports into a narrative, I realized that there is a story to tell. The ghosts of the Tenth have a story that needs to be shared. I've even found that my experiences at the Tenth could be great inspiration for fictional work. When I first decided that I was definitely going to write this book, it wasn't too long before I realized that I had made two mistakes when it came to approaching the Tenth Avenue Arts Center.

Wishing and Wanting

In hindsight, I feel that I didn't do enough historical research in the beginning. I felt there were missed moments where the team could have done something to keep the communication going when it was clear that one of the ghosts was trying to get our attention if only we had more historical information to draw on. And sometimes I kept information to myself for the sake of keeping the investigators present untainted.

I also didn't make enough trips to the Tenth, but rest assured that there will be more in the future. Certainly with the inconsistencies with the first two investigations, more than one follow-up was needed—I think visits should take place on a monthly basis, not just every few months.

There is a part of me that wishes I could go back in time and change the way things came together. But at the same time, I wouldn't take it back, as it directly affected how my relationship with the Tenth grew. The way things unfolded, as specified earlier, happened for a very distinct reason. If things went perfectly in the first place, I don't know if the experiences that ensued would have happened. Given that the investigations performed were received in different ways, it shows that the ghosts have personalities of their own that are exceptionally strong. They are very well aware that they have passed. They are very aware of their surroundings and their environment. They can also find moments to humble you: You can bring in the latest high-tech gadgets and then get no response to any questions or other methods to initiate conversation. But then, if you come into the Tenth with no tech or any kind of recording devices, the experiences flow like a massive river. The Tenth has a way of always keeping you on your toes and teaching you something new.

Sharing the Space

Since I made the decision to move away from San Diego in 2013, it forced me to research and continue my study of the Tenth from afar. From that point, as noted before, other teams began to investigate the building, which is great. More investigations at the Tenth are essential, and having a different set of eyes is crucial in the process of verifying the presence of the ghosts. Even though the Tenth has become "my baby" so to speak, keeping it all to myself will do nothing to expand the knowledge on the history and occurrences that take place. I certainly hope that I'll have the honor of being involved with other teams so I can share my passion for the building. One of the deals that APS has with Jeff is that we turn our case reports and any evidence we find over to him as soon as possible, which we always did, although sometimes it would take longer than expected.

We look at the Tenth as an ongoing case study where Jeff is the client, and witnesses are whoever wants to speak with us. If I had an unlimited budget and unlimited resources, I would bring in psychics and sketch artists and give the ghosts a face. Working with faces and names makes the ghost more human, which is what they deserve. Ghosts aren't treated like they are human primarily because we can't see them, and if they do manifest, more often than not they do not look human. I am hoping that the attitudes of the investigation field change in the next couple of years, but realistically, especially with reality television and social media, it may take more like a few decades.

With this in mind, can I ever speculate when the case will close? I suppose the case will remain open as long as Jeff will welcome my team and me into the building. Even if we are able to confirm the identities of the ghosts, it doesn't mean that the investigation is over. On the contrary, knowing the identities of the ghosts will open up many more opportunities for communication and room to experiment with different methodologies of collecting data from the past. If we can establish solid communication with the ghosts, we could possibly discover the answers to life's greatest mysteries!

I do have worries at the same time. I worry that if a ghost hunting team doesn't have any experiences on their first investigation, they could give up on the building. If APS had given up after the dull second investigation, we wouldn't have had that remarkable third trip. Also, while the first investigation was the first time APS started working on the case, it was far from my first visit there, and the events of that night were not my first paranormal experiences in the theater.

All for a Reason

Not only do I think that it is not an accident that the investigators that I met became involved, I think we were all brought together by destiny. When you have a team that investigates together, bonds are made. Connections become stronger. You begin to trust your fellow teammates with your life, and you know that they have your back, and you have theirs. The Tenth became my team's training ground—not only for the newer people, but for myself as well. We bonded in a way that we have become lifelong friends. Even though Jay, Beverly, and I moved to different parts of the country, we still stay connected and even investigate together as the old group.

Keep in mind that this team, from the first time I met them to today, has become some of the most objective investigators I have ever known. They have debunked experiences and have considered logical explanations to the point where I actually started to question whether they still believed in the paranormal. While I did have a hand in training them, they have largely developed these skills on their own. The team has studied, they ask questions, and they consider other factors before calling something paranormal. I was extraordinarily lucky to meet them and still have them on the team.

A Place Like No Other

I'm almost disappointed to say that I have yet to run into another location that is just as compelling as the Tenth Avenue Arts Center. This leads me to believe that places like this don't drop into your lap on a regular basis, so when the opportunity arises, take advantage of it. You could very well change the direction of paranormal research with a place like this.

This means using the venue for research and not just entertainment or the thrill of the hunt. If the field of investigation can change to a more research-based practice that values skills over thrills and chills, then just maybe the paranormal will get the respect that it deserves.

I do not know what the future holds for the Tenth Avenue Arts Center. It is not at risk of losing business anytime soon. The only direction I see the building going is up. And hopefully, the Tenth can also become a hub for people to explore their belief in the paranormal by having a conversation with Missy or any of the other ghosts that haunt the building.

As time goes forward, new people will be visiting the Tenth every year. If we go along with the notion that the paranormal chooses us, then I wonder who the ghosts will pick next to experience their presence. Eventually, APS will move on from the Tenth, because I know that nothing lasts forever. Whether it's because I remain away from San Diego, or I pass, or a new owner takes over the building and is not open to the paranormal, I will not be able to be a part of the Tenth's life forever. For the time being, I'm going to take advantage of the opportunity I have and cultivate it. I also hope to one day gain access to the church lofts next door, which was the site of the First Baptist Church for two of their buildings. I also want to do more research into the original site of the church on Seventh Avenue and see if there are connections between the different locations and the turbulent history of the buildings. The "White Chapel" (the church lofts), sits quietly next to the Tenth, seemingly undisturbed until someone is able to get in and do their own investigations.

The study of the Tenth Avenue Arts Center doesn't even have to stop at the paranormal. It can also be a useful facility to study parapsychology and test people who have psychic mediumship abilities. Once the identities and the presences of these ghosts are confirmed, we will have a solid foundation to build this dream upon. With so many possibilities in the theories of why the Tenth remains as haunted as it does, this is a case that won't be solved in any short period of time. And any group that claims to be able to do so is either inexperienced, or simply just full of it.

What will happen if the Tenth gets mass exposure? Only time can answer that question. Many of San Diego's numerous haunted places have been able to have teams conduct investigations without disrupting their other operations. My only hope is that the possible mass exposure will open up new opportunities and resources to solidify the history of the building. Well, maybe that is not my only hope. My other hope is that the integrity of the building and its history will remain intact. Perhaps by the time this happens, the custom of ghost hunting will have changed to be less confrontational and more respectful to the dead. Eventually, we will all join the ranks of the Tenth Avenue ghosts. As a believer in karma, I also feel that the way that we treat the deceased in life could also have the potential of affecting the state of our afterlife. Are we ready to subject ourselves to the same treatment that many ghost hunting teams put the dead through?

As other teams go through the Tenth, I hope that this book will become a resource for them and give them a starting point in moving forward, should the Tenth still be accessible for more fieldwork.

Now, here we are at the true ending of the book, which has encapsulated nearly three years of research and investigations. So many stories have come from these few years that I can't imagine what the testimonies and stories will look like in the next few years. It is exciting, but also very scary. It's a wonderful adventure that awaits us as we explore more about the other side and work toward answering that ultimate question as to where we go when we die. The general consensus is that the Tenth is haunted. The future of the building lies within us, the readers and the building's future visitors.

Now, my question to you would be ... what would you do with this chance?

The Sum of Us

As Jeff closes the theater for the evening, he looks up into the windows of the fourth floor, and with regard, he nods to the unseen faces in the glass. Whether the ghosts are actually there or not, he knows that there is something in the Tenth Avenue Arts Center. While I consider the ghosts to be my friends, he is even closer to them than anyone can imagine. From the first day he walked into the space to the end of each workday in the theater, they are watching him. They knew who he was before he was told of their stories by the church workers who were moving out of the building on that day. Truth be told, the ghosts will continue to be there long after Jeff is gone. The Tenth Avenue Arts Center is their space and their home, the place where they have chosen to spend their eternity until they finally decide to cross over into the light.

The building has weathered numerous storms, a few earthquakes, and two owners. It seems that now the Tenth is now fulfilling its purpose to the community. It went from a venue of worship to a theater where the arts are celebrated and in its own way, experiencing a form of worship. Both the participation in religion and the arts is a spiritual experience, and the Tenth has proven itself to be the perfect hub for cultivating a spiritual experience.

Even if I never go back to the Tenth, it will remain as part of my identity. That place taught me not only how to be a better playwright and actor, but also how to be a better investigator. I learned how to dig deeper into research than I ever thought possible as well as become someone who runs back into the line of fire and keeps asking those questions and engaging the presence even when I'm afraid. The ghosts at the Tenth have a story to tell, and they are looking for people to listen, especially Missy. I believe that Missy enjoys engaging with whoever is at the Tenth and is willing to pay attention to her—and, of course, she enjoys sending a few scares and thrills their way. She's more than just a child, she could very well be the most knowledgeable out of all of us as to what awaits us in the after-life. Or perhaps she is the most lost because she died at a young age and is waiting for someone to bring her mother to her to help her cross over into the light. When it comes to the British Lieutenant and the Baptist Pastor, I feel as though they are probably content being left alone, but will be okay with communicating with investigators as long as they keep it respectful. This is a hard one to figure out, as they go through moments of wanting to communicate to exuding the vibe of "leave me alone" and building the tension in the air.

Communication with the Tenth Avenue ghosts also goes a lot deeper than just rappings and EVP sessions. My investigations at the Tenth have required me to challenge myself and think outside of the box when it comes to connecting with the ghosts. There are other ways to communicate with them that disbelievers will probably shake their head at, but if someone picks up a tidbit that can't be found through a legend or a fact that has only lived in the minds of those who have been in the space, then what can the disbelievers say to that? I'm sure that the Tenth will remain a topic of controversy as well as a place where people will have an experience with the other side, whether they choose to or not. From the actors who see something moving out of the corner of their eyes to the ghost hunters who get spooked from Missy uttering a single word, they will always be there, waiting and watching over everyone.

Forever Haunted

In fact, ghosts will always remain an integral part of our existence and our identity—even for those who don't believe in them. Because whether you believe in them or not, they will always be there watching, and the ghosts of the Tenth will always be the building's watchful guardians. Silently standing by watching performances and watching people spend their workdays in their offices, they will be ever watchful and observant until someone engages with them. As they have shown, they might not always talk to you, but they can even go as far as reaching out and grabbing your leg to get your attention if they feel you are heading in the wrong direction. The concept of ghosts has both brought people together as well as torn them apart, and you must ask yourself where you fall on that scale between the two extremes of disbelief and blind belief.

If we don't believe in ghosts, then we have to figure out exactly what we do believe in. For me, I can't not believe in ghosts, because I feel like that is a form of losing faith in ourselves. The most interesting people to me are the atheists (those who don't believe in God) who believe in ghosts. If there is no God, what sort of spiritual realm exists to where ghosts are a viable possibility? Who are these ghosts accountable to? There are so many unanswered questions about the paranormal. As I have stated throughout the book, it is difficult to find tangible proof of the supernatural, but that doesn't mean that it doesn't exist. I have found that researching the past and current projects of the Rhine Research Center in Durham, North Carolina, has been a wealth of information in finding proof of the human mind's relationship with the exterior environment. Basically, this entails looking into the area of psychic abilities, which is an umbrella term for their studies in telepathy, psychokinesis, clairvoyance, and precognition, just to name a few. The Rhine has accounts of people demonstrating psychokinetic abilities, and to me, if the human mind is able to do remarkable things such as this, then wouldn't the mind, or the consciousness, have the ability to survive beyond the human body? To support this, I would argue that power is all in the mind and not dependent on the physical body. Continuing to research the Rhine and the Society of Psychical Research is a good step toward staying on top of your research and keeping up with the ever-changing theories and methodologies in the field. Bringing this research together in the Tenth Avenue Arts Center to the extent that I want to would be a dream come through. The Tenth could easily become a research center for the paranormal.

For any future guests of the Tenth, whether you are a ghost hunter, an audience member, or part of a production, I ask you to treat the space with respect—even if you don't believe in ghosts. And while respectful has become the norm, there are still a number of ghost hunters who feel that they can do whatever they want to a space, and thus, ruining it for the rest of the research field because property owners don't want to risk having their buildings damaged. I wouldn't doubt for a moment that Jeff would shut the doors to ghost hunters at the Tenth Avenue Arts Center if he felt the integrity of the building and those who use it would be compromised. Also, whether or not you believe in ghosts, don't challenge them to perform tricks, and don't provoke just for the sake of getting a response out of them. I think one of the reasons why I feel such a connection with the ghosts is that I treat them as if they are still living. The ghosts still have so much to teach us about what makes us human and much to teach us about what adventures await us after we die. If you show them respect, they will respect you in return, and maybe even want to have a bit of fun with you and your group.

As with any living human that has passed, be sure to take a moment to remember them as they were in life. I'm not saying have a full-out memorial service, but a gesture to let them know that you were thinking of them as people and not just entities for entertainment will go a long way. I truly believe that those on the other side can read our souls and our hearts and know our true intentions of being in the theater, and they can tell whether you are honorable or not. I've found that those who have gone to the Tenth and then complained to me afterward because they didn't have any sort of paranormal experience are usually partially responsible for the outcome—they either didn't respect the space, or they failed go in with an open mind. In fact, some people come with the sole purpose of trying to prove the haunting to be false. In that case, I really feel that it is a self-fulfilling prophecy. If you go in with a closed mind, you will experience nothing.

Should you decide to make a visit to the Tenth, keep in mind the things that were mentioned. Obviously, don't harass the people who work at the Tenth and don't bother the actors or production crews or whoever may be renting the location. I have found Jeff to be very easy to work with, and if you take care of the space, he will make sure that you have a good experience at the Tenth in terms of interactions with the living.

The Tenth Avenue Arts Center will always be a second home to me, therefore, I will always been extremely protective of the space not only as a haunted location, but as a performance space. Even if there were no ghosts in the building, it was a place where I got to explore myself as an actor and where I grew as a playwright as I saw my characters and my story come to life on the stage. Paranormally, it was the place where I got a step closer toward having the faith that perhaps I will survive after death and my consciousness won't cease to exist. For me, that is a gift that will continue to manifest within me, and the lessons that I learned from the Tenth will affect the way I investigate and interact with ghosts. In a sense, it has taught me how to engage with others in general, because in a sense, there are ghosts always around us, whether we see them or not. There are millions of new people born every day, but as always, there is a balance and just as many are dying each day. If those souls don't choose to move on to the light or the other side, then they are roaming this world for however long they choose. If they want to interact and engage with us as a reminder of what it was like to be alive, then it is our duty to respond in kind to elicit a productive conversation rather than provoke them and expect them to perform circus tricks. The safest approach to exploring the Tenth is to keep the golden rule in mind—treat the space and their ghosts the same way you want to be treated.

One of the Lucky Ones

To me, Jeff is extraordinarily lucky that the building is an integral part of his life and that he has access to it on a daily basis. Not only does the Tenth Avenue Arts Center play host to several ghosts, but it is also a hub for creativity and the presentation of work that reminds us what it means to exist as a human—and to not take life for granted. As he talks about the ghosts at the Tenth, you will find he speaks as if he's referring to his good friends, which I find endearing. Even though Jeff hasn't had a significant experience in the building yet, he holds significant respect for the ghosts. When I first told him about the "Mommy" incident from our first investigation, Jeff laughed and said, "Oh yes, that is Missy for you." That incident could have easily been twisted and skewed into a negative experience, but it ended up being a breakthrough moment for Jay, Rick, and myself. The paranormal doesn't always have to be foreboding. We could all take a lesson from Jeff. Instead of being fearful of the potential presences in the building, he dove in head first to seek out more information. He made the building readily available for any investigator who wanted to go in and try to communicate. I find that to be extraordinarily brave and admirable.

No matter what, I know that the building on Tenth Avenue will continue to live on—even if several decades go by and a wrecking ball takes the building down. With so much that has happened within the building's walls dating back to when First Baptist Church of San Diego owned the building combined with all the events that took place on the land and has soaked into the ground long before the foundation of the building was ever laid down, the energy will remain.

If I Should Die...

When I eventually pass, I'm fairly certain that I may want to join the realms of the theater ghosts if I have the choice. You may think I'm crazy, but theater has become such an important part of my life that I cannot imagine existing in a world where there is no art or any kind of creativity. I can't attest to what's on the other side, and as far as I know, besides a few accounts regarding near-death experiences, no one can say with 100 percent certainty that they know what is happening on the other side. I've been told that the ghosts of the Tenth enjoy watching the theatrical performances, and I know I would want to be one of those ghosts who checks in and watches a performance whenever I get the chance. Perhaps these productions serve as a reminder of what life was like before death; an opportunity to be reminiscent of a time that has long passed. And isn't that the essential nature of theater? Edward Albee once said that theater holds a mirror to society and reflects everything that we know of ourselves, both the good and the bad. To me, the Tenth Avenue Arts Center does just that by being a hub for performance and being a home to the ghosts that I've come to know so well.

So, basically what I'm trying to convey to you, my dear reader, is that the Tenth Avenue Arts Center is a place that continues to hold my fascination, and one of the few places where I feel I have established a relationship with the deceased. I feel as though I have made friends not only with Jeff and the people who use the space, but also with the unseen people who are there long after the last person leaves the building late at night. Until we are able to capture a ghost and contain it in a box, the debate will continue as to whether the Tenth is actually haunted regardless of testimony from numerous eyewitnesses and thorough examinations. Personally, I believe it is haunted, and it will take a lot to convince me otherwise. While it is disappointing that historical research hasn't been able to support the claims from the members who spoke to Jeff on move-in day, we have to keep looking at the witness testimony and keep asking questions. I especially want to keep asking the question of how and why do psychic mediums continue to pick up on the same things, such as a girl falling down the stairs (Missy), why they see a man suspended in midair (the Pastor), and why they get the sense of a military man (the British Lieutenant) barking orders in the stage area? Again, when we run into correlations and hits such as these, it underscores the fact that we need to work hard to not only confirm that there is a haunting taking place, but also try to debunk as much as possible in order to avoid going on wild goose chases.

Farewell

On my last investigation of the Tenth, I realized that in just a few months I would be starting a new life in North Carolina, and that this would potentially be my last investigation for a while. I ended up being right. As I stood in front of the building, I gazed upon the dark windows, and silently said goodbye to each ghost. I thanked them all. I said goodbye to Missy and told her to behave herself. I said goodbye to the Pastor and encouraged him to lay down his burden of guilt and move on to the light. I said goodbye to the British Lieutenant and told him that he no longer had to stay at the Tenth in order to remain spiritual. I also said goodbye to the unnamed ghosts that had yet to identify themselves; the little boy in the wine cellar and the dark shadow in the Fourth-Floor Theater (which was renamed the Forum Theater in 2015). I became emotional in my goodbye and found my eyes getting wet with tears. As I turned my back to leave, I found myself stopping and looking over my shoulder to the windows above. If I didn't know any better, each of them may have been at the windows watching as I walked further away from them; leaving them to wait for the next person to give them their attention and waiting to let their voices be heard.

Are you ready to listen?

To Write the Author

If you wish to contact the author or would like more information about this book, please write to the author in care of Llewellyn Worldwide, and we will forward your request. Both the author and publisher appreciate hearing from you and learning of your enjoyment of this book and how it has helped you. Llewellyn Worldwide cannot guarantee that every letter written to the author can be answered, but all will be forwarded. Please write to:

Alex Matsuo
℅ Llewellyn Worldwide
2143 Wooddale Drive
Woodbury, MN 55125-2989

Please enclose a self-addressed stamped envelope for reply, or $1.00 to cover costs. If outside the USA, enclose an international postal reply coupon.

GET MORE AT LLEWELLYN.COM

Visit us online to browse hundreds of our books and decks, plus sign up to receive our e-newsletters and exclusive online offers.

- • Free tarot readings • Spell-a-Day • Moon phases
- • Recipes, spells, and tips • Blogs • Encyclopedia
- • Author interviews, articles, and upcoming events

GET SOCIAL WITH LLEWELLYN

Find us on
Facebook

www.Facebook.com/LlewellynBooks

Follow us on
twitter™

www.Twitter.com/Llewellynbooks

GET BOOKS AT LLEWELLYN

LLEWELLYN ORDERING INFORMATION

Order online: Visit our website at www.llewellyn.com to select your books and place an order on our secure server.

Order by phone:
- • Call toll free within the U.S. at 1-877-NEW-WRLD (1-877-639-9753)
- • Call toll free within Canada at 1-866-NEW-WRLD (1-866-639-9753)
- • We accept VISA, MasterCard, and American Express

Order by mail:
Send the full price of your order (MN residents add 6.875% sales tax) in U.S. funds, plus postage and handling to: Llewellyn Worldwide, 2143 Wooddale Drive, Woodbury, MN 55125-2989

POSTAGE AND HANDLING:

STANDARD: (U.S. & Canada)
(Please allow 12 business days)
$25.00 and under, add $4.00.
$25.01 and over, FREE SHIPPING.

INTERNATIONAL ORDERS (airmail only):
$16.00 for one book, plus $3.00 for each additional book.

Visit us online for more shipping options.
Prices subject to change.

FREE CATALOG!

To order, call
1-877-
NEW-WRLD
ext. 8236
or visit our
website

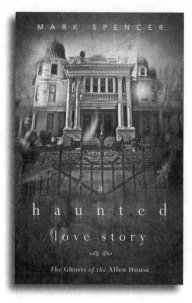

A Haunted Love Story
The Ghosts of the Allen House
MARK SPENCER

A Haunted Love Story is two tales in one: a modern family's attempt to embrace their strange, spirit-inhabited home and a vintage love affair kept secret for six decades.

When Mark Spencer bought the beautiful old Allen House in Monticello, Arkansas, he knew that it was famously haunted. According to ghost lore, the troubled spirit of Ladell Allen, who mysteriously committed suicide in the master bedroom in 1948, still roamed the historic mansion. Yet Mark remained skeptical—until he and his family began witnessing faceless phantoms, a doppelganger spirit, and other paranormal phenomena. Ensuing ghost investigations offered convincing evidence that six spirits, including Ladell, inhabited their home. But the most shocking event occured the day Mark followed a strange urge to explore the attic and found, crammed under a floorboard, secret love letters that touchingly depict Ladell Allen's forbidden, heart-searing romance—and shed light on her tragic end.

978-0-7387-3073-8, 240 pp., 5³⁄₁₆ x 8 **$15.95**

To order, call 1-877-NEW-WRLD
Prices subject to change without notice
Order at Llewellyn.com 24 hours a day, 7 days a week

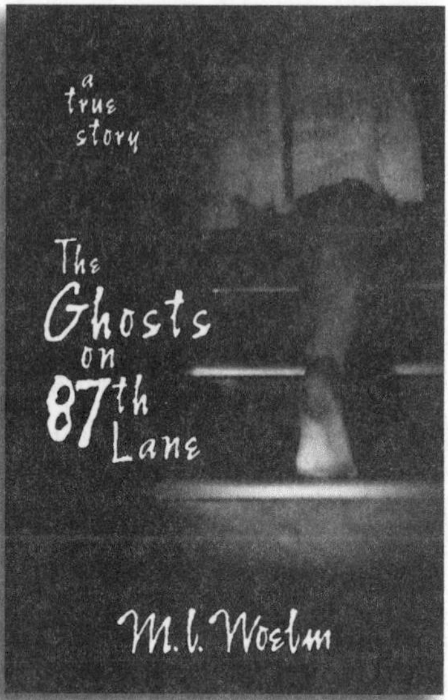
a true story
The Ghosts on 87th Lane
M. L. Woelm

The Ghosts on 87th Lane
A True Story
M. L. Woelm

After moving her young family into their first house—a small suburban home in the Midwest—a series of strange and chilling events take place: unexplained noises, objects disappearing, lights going out by themselves, phantom footsteps. And then M. L. Woelm's neighbor confirms the horrifying truth: her house is haunted.

Beginning in 1968 and spanning three decades, this moving memoir chronicles the hair-raising episodes that nearly drove an ordinary housewife and mother to the breaking point. With friends who thought she was crazy and a skeptical, unsupportive husband who worked nights, the author was left all alone in her terror. How did she cope with disembodied sobs, eerie feelings of being watched, mysterious scratches appearing on her throat, and a phantom child's voice crying "Mommy!" in her ear?

Discover how frazzled nerves and constant stress wreak havoc on the author's health and marriage, until she finally finds validation and understanding from ghost expert Echo Bodine, friends, her grown children, and finally... her husband.

978-0-7387-1031-0, 288 pp., 6 x 9   **$12.95**

To order, call 1-877-NEW-WRLD
Prices subject to change without notice
Order at Llewellyn.com 24 hours a day, 7 days a week

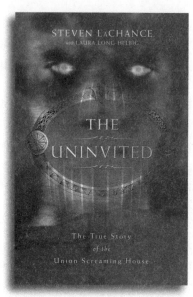

STEVEN LaCHANCE
with LAURA LONG HELBIG

THE

UNINVITED

The True Story
of the
Union Screaming House

The Uninvited
The True Story of the Union Screaming House
STEVEN A. LACHANCE

Its screams still wake me from sleep. I see the faceless man standing in that basement washing away the blood from his naked body.

Steven LaChance was forever transformed by the paranormal attacks that drove him and his family from their home in Union, Missouri. When another family falls victim to the same dark entity, Steven returns to the dreaded house to offer aid and find healing.

Paranormal investigators, psychics, and priests are consulted, but no relief is found. The demon's presence—screams, growls, putrid odors, invisible shoves, bites, and other physical violations—only grow worse. LaChance chronicles how this supernatural predator infects those around it. But the one who suffers most is the current homeowner, Helen. When the entity takes possession and urges Helen toward murder and madness, LaChance must engage in a hair-raising battle for her soul.

The Uninvited is a true and terrifying tale of extreme haunting, demon possession, and an epic struggle between good and evil.

978-0-7387-1357-1, 264 pp., 6 x 9   **$16.95**

To order, call 1-877-NEW-WRLD
Prices subject to change without notice
Order at Llewellyn.com 24 hours a day, 7 days a week

The Sallie House Haunting
A True Story
DEBRA PICKMAN

Debra Pickman moved with her family into the now notorious Sallie House. Sallie is the young ghost haunting the house. At first, it's just poltergeist-like mischief. Toys turn on by themselves. Small items are moved. The electricity is disrupted. And then things take a chilling turn.

Although Debra likes Sallie, she can't prevent her from starting fires. When her husband Tony is attacked with scratches and bites, it becomes obvious there is more than just Sallie there—there is an evil presence that is taking over the house. Soon full apparitions and violent attacks take a toll on their family, culminating in the terror that finally drives them away.

The Sallie House has been featured on numerous TV shows, and here for the first time, Debra Pickman recounts the whole story of the haunting that changed her family's life. Included are photos and transcripts of EVP recordings.

978-0-7387-2128-6, 288 pp., 6 x 9　　　　　　　　**$16.95**

To order, call 1-877-NEW-WRLD
Prices subject to change without notice
Order at Llewellyn.com 24 hours a day, 7 days a week